Prunes and Prism

PRUNES AND PRISM

WITH OTHER ODDS AND ENDS

BY

Charles Hall Grandgent

Essay Index Reprint Series

BOOKS FOR LIBRARIES PRESS

FREEPORT, NEW YORK

INTERNATIONAL STANDARD BOOK NUMBER:
0-8369-2227-1

LIBRARY OF CONGRESS CATALOG CARD NUMBER:
70-128251

PRINTED IN THE UNITED STATES OF AMERICA

Preface

IN behalf of the following meditations and narratives
I can urge only the plea that it is their first offence.
None have seen the light before, except the first essay, a
great part of which appeared in the *Harvard Graduates'
Magazine* for March, 1927, and the little study of *Benjamin
Franklin the Reformer*, printed in *The Scholastic*, May 28,
1927.

C. H. GRANDGENT

CAMBRIDGE, MASSACHUSETTS
October, 1927

Contents

Prunes and Prism

Prunes and Prism

"**P**APA, potatoes, poultry, prunes and prism, all very good words for the lips, — especially prunes and prism." Thus spake the prim governess in *Little Dorrit*. I have forgotten her name; if you must have specific data, let me refer you to Book II, Chapter V. But the important thing is not her name, or her book and chapter, but her doctrine, which reaches much further than she ever suspected. You remember, no doubt, that the prunish and prismatic pedagogue aforesaid, by training her young lady charges to keep constantly in mind the aforesaid vocables, inculcated in them an expression of propriety and a demeanor of decorum. Thus far she was right; but her instruction, though she knew it not, went beyond the outward signs of propriety: her formula inevitably developed not only the show but the spirit of decorum. For our spirit is shaped by its manifestations, our thought is determined by the words we use.

How can it be otherwise? We think with words, we cannot put together the tiniest notion without them. Words are the stuff of which our cogitations are made; and the words which happen to be in vogue at a particular time and place determine the ideas which are then and there current. I do not deny that there is a reciprocal influence. The character, the civilization of a community must have some causative effect on its vocabulary. Such action, however, is very deep down, and, despite (or because of) the labors of psychological philologists, it resists most attempts to bring it into the light of day. Whereas the opposite process is as plain as daylight to everybody. Some fellow invents a word — or, if he does not really create it, gives it a use. Either the fellow is a prominent fellow or his invention strikes people's fancy; other fellows imitate the first fellow, and still others copy them, until a mode of thought is established for a whole generation.

Examples crowd upon us. To begin with something close at hand, consider the term "student activities," which, as you know, indicates everything that a student does, except study. Now, when you and I were in college, we worked a part of the time and played a part of the time, in proportions that differed according to your proclivities and mine. But, whether or not our playtime was most of our daytime (if I may indulge in a Swinburnian rime), we called our play, "play," or "fun" or "sport" or "amusement"; and none of those designations spoiled the pleasure of the thing or compelled us to look upon it as one of the serious businesses of life. *Mais nous avons changé tout cela.* Since the invention of the portentous expression, "student activities," the frothy lightness has evaporated and sport as well as study has become a horrid grind. In one of our big institutions, when there was proposed a system of concentration calling for increased effort in the closing year, the local undergraduate journal argued against its adoption, because it was likely to interfere with the "Senior student activities" — meaning thereby, as far as I could make out, certain functional dances which formed a part of the unwritten Senior curriculum. Making all allowance for the high seriousness of youth, is it conceivable that the youthful journalist would have argued thus about "Senior amusements"? No: naught but the baleful word "activities" could have betrayed anyone into such solemnity.

Without quitting the precincts of pedagogy, answer me another question: "Do you know what is meant by the *coëfficient of correlation?*" Neither do I, but I have constantly to look as if I did, because one cannot read or hear a paragraph of pedagogical discussion without encountering it. From frequent rubbing up against the phrase, I have come to gain a dim notion of its message; I fancy it signifies the degree of correspondence between two tables of figures, or something of that sort. But my point is this: since the introduction of that term, pedagogy has ceased to be a matter of pure nomenclature, and has become a matter of mathematics. I defy anyone to keep the "coëfficient of correlation" on his tongue's end and talk of anything otherwise than mathematically. Just look into any new book in the field, and you will find it a mere mass of statistics. Now, it was not thus before the transmogrifying formula was invented. In those days, all that one needed was to learn by heart certain turns of expression. One of my colleagues, many years ago, was about to seek a certificate to teach in the schools of New York, and came to me in some trepidation about his examinations — or rather, about one of them; he was well up in all the subjects except Education, which he had never studied at all. I told him to be of good heart: the answers to the questions would be easy enough for a man of intelligence; but he must be sure to make use of the right phrases. And I wrote him a list of a score of them, which I exhorted him to shove in whenever reason or rime should permit. He did so, and came off with flying colors. But he could not do it now: the "coëfficient of correlation" would get him. I wonder whether the same story, *mutatis mutandis*, might not be told of other arts and sciences.

There was a time when, if you hit a man, he either turned the other cheek or slugged you in the jaw; and, after recovering from the shock which either response occasioned, you judged his character accordingly. That is, you estimated his deeds in terms of human nature, because you had not yet become familiar with the word "reaction." The prevalence of this designation now obliges us to take a chemical attitude toward the conduct of our fellow creatures. Slugging in the jaw is one reaction, turning the other cheek is a different reaction, to the same stimulus. There is no question of good or bad, of moral or immoral, not even of "ethical" or "unethiçal" (as the preferred phraseology now runs); there is nothing but mechanical sequence of one motion upon another. So it is when you read a book or see a play or hear a concert: it does not stir an emotion in you or leave an impression; it excites a reaction. Morality and sentiment are turned to chemistry.

Perhaps you think that you have a shrinking disposition. You are mistaken: what you have is an "inferiority complex." If Emerson were now writing his essay on "English Traits," he would have to call it "English Complexes." Dispositions, traits, characteristics have left us, like the "humors" and "vapors" of an earlier generation, and complexes are not only the chief of our diet, but our whole bill of fare. When you and I were young was the time to commit murder, but we did not know it, and I (perhaps you also) missed the chance. At present, to assassinate with impunity, one must be either rich or crazy; in that golden age the opportunity was open to the poorest and sanest. The only requisite was filial affection. No matter how heinous your crime, how black your record, how callous your conscience, you had your cell filled with flowers, you were coddled by sympathetic ladies, you drew tears from the jury, and you always got off, if it could be shown that you were "kind to your mother." Kindness to mother was the universal exculpator. Ah! how often we have heard, in the dear old Saturnian days: "He is not altogether a good boy, I fear, but his heart is in the right place; he is kind to his mother." And everybody thought better of the young sinner in question than they thought of the young saint whose devotion to his mother was less conspicuous. Now it is too late. It is useless for the criminal to be kind to his mother: for that kindness simply means an "Oedipus complex," which wins him no sympathy at all.

Oedipus, I dare say, was "oversexed." At any rate, that is the modern term for unchaste; and, as you will easily see, it carries with it not so much a leveling of valuations as an inversion of them. The elderly man who, when finally prosperous, deserts the partner of his toils, and runs off with a pretty-faced typewriter, is not to be blamed, but rather envied: he is "oversexed" — a natural attribute for which he is no more responsible than for the presence or absence of a good head of hair or a full set of teeth. On the other hand, those impostors, Joseph and Sir Galahad, who have so long been held up as models to our dutiful admiration, owe all their reputation to the accident of being "undersexed."

According to the rhetoric of the moment, it is improper to construct a sentence, or even a phrase, that does not contain the word "sex." The selling factor of a best seller used to be a love story; now it is a "sex problem." The "heart interest," which was the trump card of the drama, has become a "sex conflict." The woman who used to have "feminine charm" now has "sex appeal." If the relation of electron to proton has not yet become a "sex relation," it is only because the sex-mongers have been too busy with sex-mongering to follow the progress of electrical science. Inasmuch as the word "sex" enters into every factor on each side of every equation, why not eliminate it and save ourselves just so much breath and so much ink? I have forgotten the name of that clergyman who finally checked a tiresomely profane young man with the remark: "Let us assume, once for all, that everything and everybody is damned, and proceed on that basis." Thus perish all witless and wearisome parrots!

If the color of sex has come to pervade all our thinking, even as the smell of gasoline forms the major constituent of our atmosphere, we owe that ether-like omnipresence, in great measure, to a Viennese nerve-doctor called by some of his American disciples "Froude." Now, there is in one of this Austrian's books — his "Interpretation of Dreams" — an anecdote which I have never seen quoted anywhere. I found it in the book itself; for, unlike many Freudians, I have read several works by the master. The story occurs in the elucidation of a dream dreamt by the author, wherein appears the figure of Hannibal. If I remember rightly, something that had happened within twenty-four hours had suggested a childish experience of Freud's, and this infantile occurrence was associated in the dreamer's mind with the great Carthaginian. The latter, you know, once swore to his father, Hamilcar, an awful vengeance against the Romans. And that event had connected itself with the following incident in Freud's early years. His father was telling him of a new hat which he, the father, when a young man, had paraded with pardonable satisfaction along the street; but his pride had had a rude fall when a stranger, with the comment, "That hat is too good for a Jew," had snatched the offending article from his head and thrown it into the mud. "What did you do then, father?" asked the horrified and indignant boy. "I picked my hat from the mud and walked quietly away." Then it was (he tells us) that the youthful Freud registered an oath of vengeance against the Christians. How successfully he has kept his vow!

This Freud, perhaps, has supplied us with more disturbing words than any other writer since Jean-Jacques Rousseau. The Genevan, however, interested though he was in sex, has been dominant rather in our social and political vocabulary. To him we owe the popularity of "natural goodness," of "back to nature," of "the iniquity of private property," of "education by experience," of "government by the consent of the governed." You may be glad to know that a student, in a written examination, once gave me a curious illustration of our philosopher's inconsistency. Alas! which of mankind, even the most oversexed, can always attune practice to principle? "At about this time," began the student — no time having been previously mentioned. "At about this time," by the way, is a favorite opening for studentdom, provided no date be in sight, before or after. Its advantage, under these circumstances, is that it gives an appearance of chronological attachment, while remaining absolutely detached and non-committal. Of course, had a figure preceded, the phrase had been all too venturesome; without a figure, it is safe, though illusory. However, why criticize the student for his caution? What better quality can education inculcate? Besides, if the young man were capable of discoursing interminably about matters to him unknown, he ought to be, not a student, but a professor. Be that as it may, the youth in question wrote as follows: "At about this time lived Jean-Jacques Rousseau, a reformer who gave parents much good advice which he neglected to follow, himself — for instance, that they should nurse their own children."

Was Rousseau a Radical or a Reactionary? Or a Radical-Reactionary or a Reactionary-Radical? Our conception of the thing depends on the name which the fashion of the day happens to dictate. The face of Freedom changes expression according as we call it Liberalism, Democracy, Radicalism, Socialism, Communism, or Anarchy, although all these terms have been used, in various times and places, to designate simply the freer of two contending parties. One of the best cartoons I ever saw was in a French paper of the eighties. Two elderly gentlemen are gazing sadly at a shrunken, dilapidated old Jezebel, who is labeled "Madame la République"; and one is saying to the other: "Ah! qu'elle était belle sous l'Empire!"

In the jargon of politics, one of the most potent slogans is "—— for the ——s." At the opening of the first Egyptian parliament in Cairo, I heard the cry: "Egypt for the Egyptians!" It was not boisterous or insistent, but its repetition ultimately led to assassination, which, in turn, brought worse subjection. In Constantinople, at the time when the Sultan was deposed, I surmised rather than heard the sentiment: "Turkey for the Turks!" This principle came to mean the expulsion of all outlanders from the public service, and even the gradual exclusion of all foreign residents from the country, as far as this could be accomplished without too violently jarring Turkey's reputation. For the New Turks are very sensitive, deeply hurt by the ill opinion of occidental peoples, especially ours. "Turkey is a sadly misunderstood nation," said one of them to me, pathetically.

With us, "America for the Americans" has produced, among other things, the Ku Klux Klan. I know a village whose population is as nearly homogeneous as a population of several hundred can be. Honest, hard-working, hospitable, kindly people they all are, far from fanatical yet not distinctly irreligious. Among them are no Jews, no Negroes, and only two Catholics — both of them highly esteemed citizens. Yet this community must have its lodge of the K. K. K., to which a considerable proportion of the men belong. The only activity of the organization would seem to be to stir up dissension where none existed before. The two Catholics are not molested, and probably have no fear of molestation, yet they must find it hard to think charitably of a gang whose theoretical purpose is to persecute them. It is not they, however, who are loud in denunciation of the Klan; its fiercest enemies are men of the Klan's own blood and church. Most vehement among them is Captain Bill, a veteran of the Civil War. "One hundred per cent American, they call themselves! I call 'em one hundred per cent damn fools. Just foolishness and trouble-makin', that's all it is. I won't hev nothin' to do with 'em. I hef to git all my groceries in Heckville, because I won't trade with no damn Klansman. An' I hef to go ten miles to git my hair cut, because both our barbers belong to the Klan."

No one can doubt Captain Bill's patriotism. At the time of the World War, being then nearly eighty, he bewailed his enforced abstention. "What a fool notion it is," he would say, "to take off the young fellers, that might be a-farmin', and leave the old men, that can't do nothin' but set around. Why! I ain't no good at all a-workin', but I could set in a trench just as good as anybody." At last it was too much for him, and he made a determined effort to enlist, presenting himself for physical examination. After which formality the inspector thus solemnly addressed him: "If you want us to take you, Captain Bill, you'll hef to bring us the written consent of your parents."

But why does our model village, despite the denunciation of its hundred-per-centest American, maintain a lodge? I think I know the answer; and you can guess it, too, if you call to mind the prosaic monotony of everyday life in a Yankee hamlet. Hard work and little fun; and, above all, little food for the innate love of romance. No song, no festival, no spectres, no fairies, no demons. The charm of the Klan lies, not in its principles, but in its weirdness and mystery. Remember how, as a child, you delighted in everything secret — secret societies, secret meeting-places, a secret language, secret signals, a secret post-office, the secret service. Remember how deliciously your flesh crept and your nerves tingled at the word. Now, here you have a nation-wide underground association, bursting with secrecy, abounding in ghostly ceremonial and grotesque titles. What childlike soul, starving for poetry, could resist its lure?

For the Yankee soul is childlike. It wants its newspaper full of pictures; it revels in a "comic strip"; it requires on the front page of its journal bigger type than any other people craves. One day, seated at a third-story window on Tremont St., and looking across at the northeast corner of the Boston Common, I saw there a dog

carrying in his mouth a newspaper, whose scare headings
I could easily read at that distance; and I am not an
eagle. It really seemed that the journal must have been
intended for the intelligence of the dog that held it, rather
than for the mind of his master. If the K. K. K. ever
loses its klutch on such simplicity, the instrument of its
downfall will be, not ratiocination, but the radio.

The radio, indeed, has taken a greater hold here than
anywhere else, and no wonder. So did the "movie," when
it was new. So does the automobile. It is characteristic
of the simple mind to carry every object of interest to the
extreme, to run every fancy into the ground. The experienced man is chary of playing with a child, because he
knows that when once a game is started, his infantile partner will never want to stop. But the sports of our nation's
adolescent and adult cannot rest, either, until they have
grown into manias. We cannot be satisfied with fun; we
must turn it into the most anxious business of life. What
devotee was ever more enslaved to his divinity than the
baseball fan, unless it be the golf fiend? Even thus it
goes with other things. One year, we cannot be kicked
into war, bearing an abominable series of insults and out-
rages with a beatific smile; the next year we go to fighting
with the sustained frenzy of a Moslem, we make illegal
the sale of books in the enemy's language, we pursue with
suspicion everyone with a foreign name, we make the
mildest expostulation a crime, and we keep up our belli-
cose attitude, our warlike intolerance long after hostilities
have ceased. We cannot drink without getting drunk,
and consequently we cannot keep sober without going
dry. Such is the simple mind, which pursues with un-
questioning persistency the *ignis fatuus* of a catch-word.

We are fond of children; no quality can be more engaging, not even kindness to one's mother. But whither, in our follow-up tendency, do we carry that amiable tenderness? So fond are we that we cannot bear to see the little ones even momentarily thwarted, we cannot bear to see them do anything reluctantly, we cannot bear to see them cry. "He's nothing but a child" reconciles us to every delinquency short of murder — and occasionally leads even to that. "He's nothing but a child" makes us unwilling to allow him really to exert himself in his preparation for maturity, and we devise all manner of procrastination and painless pedagogy for the longest possible postponement of the evil day when he shall have to use his poor little brain. As dances and rides and games increase, so do study hours necessarily dwindle. The outcome has been, except for the uncollegiate proletariat, a prolongation of childhood until the age of twenty-two, that being the time when the dear infant graduates from the high school which we indulgently call a "college." We have been told, indeed, that in mankind the development of the family, and hence of civilization, is due to the long duration of infancy, with its helplessness, its need of unremitting parental care. That is a beautiful thought and doubtless a true one. But have we not overdone it in our country? Really, twenty-two years out of the allotted three score and ten seems an exorbitant proportion for incubation. And I cannot see that with the stretching of the puerile period there has come a correspondingly increased refinement in the product. Are our present-day young men and young women, hatched at twenty-two, notably more civilized than the young of other lands, where the chicks leave the shell at eighteen? Perhaps we have reached the stage of diminishing returns.

At any rate, our young people seem to think so. For a

reaction has set in; and it seems to proceed not so much from the overfond parent as from the overfondled child. Fresh catch-words have gained currency, such as "service," "leadership," "aggressiveness," which have led to a more literal understanding of Roosevelt's long-ago phrase, "the strenuous life." For many years "the strenuous life," as far as our undergraduates were concerned, meant wearing a slouch hat, smoking a pipe, and watching other people play billiards. But new words and new events have largely discredited such a free interpretation of the motto and have brought into vogue an exegesis more in accordance with the principles of fundamentalism. We are regaled with the not infrequent spectacle of American collegians who take in doing something the same pleasure which their predecessors took in doing nothing. Idling time, which used to seem to studentdom the only real time, is shrinking to modest proportions in the bright calendar of youth. Where are the long, lazy, sunshiny summer vacations to which we look back with mingled wonder and ecstasy? Take a look at the summer hotels, once swarming with husky, leisurely lads, now inhabited by lonely ladies and debilitated old gentlemen.

Among Harvard alumni was voiced, last year, much indignant protest over the abandonment of our old commons in Memorial Hall. Randall Hall had, to be sure, long since banished its consumers, without mourning; but it had possessed none of the endearing associations of the elder refectorium. Stronger than its smells, mellower than its meats, were the joys of Memorial commensality. Why, then, was the great hall closed? Simply because the students would not eat there any longer. But why should they be unwilling to take their meals in spacious ease amidst congenial company? Because they could not afford the time. What they prefer is the quickest of quick service in the nearest spot, and nourishment rapid of digestion and moderate in amount. Therefore do they betake themselves to the "one-arm joint," even as you and I. The very Freshmen, compelled to eat in their own attractive dormitories, which are especially contrived to foster social habits, gulp down their rations and rush away, often without exchanging a word. Also those numerous upper-classmen who seek their own clubs at mealtimes have ceased to linger, even metaphorically, over their nuts and wine. To be busy, incessantly busy, is now the ideal, as it was once the undergraduate's dream to be uninterruptedly unoccupied.

Therein are the sons much like the fathers. How many clubmen now really loiter about the clubhouse? As I see them, they run in to telephone, to glance at the headings in the paper, often to attend a business luncheon, and then are gone, presumably to another club to do the same things there. Clubs, I am told, are nowadays so numerous that, with the best will in the world, an individual clubman cannot give more than a few minutes a week to each. A conscientious club-hound will of course do his best; indeed, it is remarkable what some of them, even the obscurest, will accomplish. Of course such people can have no homes. Would you achieve immortality? Here is a safe recipe: become an obscure clubman. Let me explain. Take up the *Transcript*, and on the front page you see: "Death of Prominent Clubman." Look at the *Herald:* "Death of Prominent Clubman." The *Globe* displays the same legend; so does the *American*. But have you ever seen the notice: "Death of Obscure Clubman?" Not once in your life. They never die. Become, then, a mute, inglorious clubman, and devote your life to a vain but worthy attempt to get the worth of your dues out of as many clubs as there are days.

In one of them, perhaps, you will get a satisfactory breakfast. At any rate, you will stand a better chance than you would have at a hotel. If I had capital, and were to begin my career anew, I should run a hotel and should make a point of furnishing prompt, hot, and wholesome Sunday breakfasts. Breakfast-time is just the moment when the guest needs the promptest, hottest, and wholesomest treatment; and it is just the moment when he is most neglected. Early morning — the sad seedy hour, when one is all nerves and irritability and emptiness, and for the most part in a desperate hurry. You enter the dark breakfast-room and drop into a chair near a window, if there is one, under the guidance of a comparatively plump and prosperous attendant, who thereafter disappears from your life. Around the outskirts of the hall flit ghostlike a few emaciated wrecks, in misfit evening costume, who look even sicker than you feel. You wonder vaguely what distant country saw their birth (assuming that they were born) and what language they speak, if they speak at all. This topic of conjecture is wellnigh exhausted, when one of them draws near and dumps upon your table, with a heavy thud, a morning paper four inches thick. Then he, too, vanishes forever from the scene. The one thing these people do swiftly is to vanish. I suppose they die; but they contrive somehow to do it off-stage, as in the Classic drama. It would stimulate a languid but rather pleasurable interest if, as in the red-blooded Shakesperean play, they would expire right before you. However, in them, life is so close to death that the transition could furnish little excitement.

They must crawl off and die in the walls; and you picture to yourself the mural hollows filled with their desiccated corpses. After a considerable era, during which your imagination has thus peopled all the possible parietal interstices, it occurs to you to look at the paper. One really might as well try to read the telephone book — better, indeed, for it would be easier to handle. You pick up one section, and three or four other sections drop out of it on the floor. At last you get a wad of it propped up on the table and detect among the headlines a murder that may justify pursuit through half a column — though certainly not into section F, page 16, column 4. At this moment you become aware of something that seems to be in motion. It is one of the ghouls. You cannot actually see him move, yet somehow you are sure that the black lines of his spectrum, if you could watch them, would show the spectre to be approaching. In the course of time he is at your side, armed with pencil and memorandum pad, and holds before you a formidable card, on which are inscribed innumerable nauseous and indigestible aliments. While your bewildered gaze wanders over it, vainly groping for a flash of inspiration, the spectre stands silent and immobile, not looking at anything in particular. His hand holds the pencil in readiness but there is no speculation in his eyes. Finally you order grapefruit, coffee, and dry toast; and the spectre vanishes like his predecessors. After a while you begin to wonder whether you ever really saw him at all. The other ghosts have faded away, too. You are alone in the great dark hall. A faint ray of light penetrates from somewhere. Perhaps it is dawn; perhaps cockcrow has put all the wraiths to rout. And you sit and dream.

For the sequel, see section F, page 16, column 4. What

you have lived through is a survival from a bygone age, before everybody had a haste-complex. Our present existences have really only two experiences left to remind us of that period: the hotel breakfast and the Sunday paper. Perhaps, instead of impatience, I should visit gratitude upon them; for they alone resist the overmastering delusion of our generation, the delusion that we are always in a hurry. It is a curious madness, when you come to think of it, this idea that the universe depends on our never losing a second. Most of us, most of the time, are doing things of no special importance; whether we do them this minute or next makes little difference even to ourselves, and none to anybody else. The hotel breakfast and the Sunday paper soothe us back into a sense of our insignificance, standing, as they do, the one for infinity of time, the other for infinity of space. What are all our little hurries and worries compared to these serene immensities? In their presence all of us — the artist with his self-expression-complex, the critic with his superiority-complex, the business man with his tire-complex — should have one and the same reaction: sleep.

The haste-mania, no doubt, furnishes additional proof of that childishness of which I have spoken. How the little boy loves to plunge downhill on his sled! But not more than the rube enjoys the thrill of shooting the chutes at Coney Island, or the roadhog savors the ecstasy of blind lightning flight in his automobile. The desire to go fast, just for the sake of going fast, is primitive, however sophistical be our justification of it. There is good in it, too, if we regard occidental culture as a good thing. I suspect it has had something to do with the recent vitalization of the American student. The speed-complex may be held for a while in partial subjection by such words as "prunes" and "prism," but is again stirred to self-assertion by explosive terms like "pep," "punch," and "guts." You must admit that between the language used by the young and the nature of their student activities there is a high coëfficient of correlation.

One reason why the Neanderthal type of man delights in speed and why the rustic revels in the Ku Klux Klan, is that they lack imagination. With them, physical flight has to take the place of fancy's wing. We think of imagination as a primitive trait, which fades with increase of knowledge; but this does not seem to be true. Imagination, to be sure, is inborn, and it is most active in the child, who of necessity, even among the wildest people, is being educated at a rate never afterwards approached; but it is soon stunted if not fed. The superstitions of savages, which to our blasé mind seem at first so romantic, are, on closer examination, dull and stupid things — originally, perhaps, childish absurdities that in adult repetition have forfeited all their spontaneity and all their charm. The whole life of the savage, as far as it can be understood by the stay-at-home observer, is one everlasting routine of wearisome ceremonial, one senseless sequence of cut-and-dried observances, which, if they ever had a real meaning, evidently lost it at some forgotten stage. If primitive adult man had possessed imagination, he would not have remained so long in the Neanderthal condition, only to die out eventually and make room for a new race that did not allow imagination to become atrophied so early. The young of animals — notably kittens and puppies — display imagination in their sports, but reveal only occasional flashes of it when they are grown. So it is with the common type of man.

It is a mistake to conceive of the ignorant as imagina-

tive and of the learned as matter-of-fact. Put this view
to the test by actually tapping members of the two
classes, and its falsity will be clear. It is almost the opposite of the truth. Almost, but not quite; for the matter-of-fact are not necessarily the ignorant, but those who
are not rising out of their ignorance; and the imaginative
are not so much the learned as those who have not ceased
to learn. Imagination is both a cause and an effect of
progress; it is a by-product of education, whether the
education be that of Dame Nature or of the Dames'
School. As long as novelties are flowing in, the mind is
kept alert; the picturing and inventing processes are in
full swing. When one reaches the stage where the day
brings nothing that is unaccustomed, the creative faculty
begins to wither. The poet is he who is forever surprised,
he who is continually seeing something new. Every child
is a poet, and every poet is a child: this is true if we take
the word "poet" etymologically, letting it describe every
constructive genius, the inventor as well as the sonneteer.
The prosaic mind is the mind which has forgotten how to
be astonished, having reduced to formulas all the phenomena it observes, or having ceased to observe any that
are not formulated. It is the speakers of prose, like Mon-
sieur Jourdain, who are most subject to the tyranny of
the current word.

Imagination is the mainspring of human progress. In
fact, I can think of no other primal motive power, except
accident. And even when accident gave the start, imagination was needed to develop the consequences. It was
an accident of man's physical structure that he was able
to talk; but his adaptation of that faculty to his own purposes has been the work of his own inventiveness. Accident, no doubt, kindled the first fire before the startled

eyes of human beings, and continued to kindle it time and time again before a startled brain conceived the notion of making fire a servitor; but think of all that man has gradually extracted from that notion! The longest step is not the imitative burning of a house to roast the pig, but the discovery that the porker can be roasted without the sacrifice of a dwelling. Speech and the use of fire are mankind's two fundamental inventions. And the greater of these, speech, after liberating man from the thraldom of nature, has, as we have seen, subjected our kind to its own tyranny.

But that subjection need not be noxious, if only we keep imagination alive. The inhabitants of Erewhon, you remember, rose up, just in time, against the tyranny of machines, and abolished them. We need not be so radical; nor could we, if we would. Language, man's greatest creation, has come to stay; for it has enabled him to think consecutively, and in giving him that power, has deprived him of the liberty of thinking at all without its aid. I cannot protest against speech, vocally, visually, or mentally, without protesting in speech's own terms. But I can prevent speech from turning my ideas, and consequently my conduct, to pure automatism, if I nourish fitly my capacity for surprise. One might guess, offhand, that the less a creature knows, the oftener that creature is surprised; but the very reverse is true. I doubt whether a clam is ever astonished at anything except its own violent death by overheating; and that experience comes in every instance too late to permit imagination to invent a remedy. A rabbit, which indubitably knows more than a clam, has frequent occasion for surprise, if one may judge from its expression. And a poet, more knowing than a hare (though just as mad), lives, as I have already said, in a state of perpetual wonderment. Now, it is the poet, above all other creatures, who triumphs over the absolutism of language. He it is who makes speech a servant, instead of a master, just as the general run of mankind has subjugated fire — although it must be confessed that in both cases the domineering element occasionally escapes from human control.

The moral is this: cultivate the habit of surprise, to keep the imagination green; for imagination alone can save us from ossification of the head. The really cultivated mind is never too old for amazement. "Pray, tell me, your Grace," asked the indiscreet young man who had succeeded in getting himself presented to the Duke of Wellington, "is it true that you were surprised at Waterloo?" "No," answered the Iron Duke, "but I am now." After all he had seen — or rather because of all he had seen and understood — Wellington was still capable of wonder.

To understand and to wonder, to wonder and to understand: these are our soul's needs; and these should be the goal of our education. But how can wonderment be taught? It is not a question of teaching, of imparting; it is a question of sustaining. The faculty is there, eager to live, but craving novelty to live on. As long as we continue adding to our store ever new things and ever more that is new, so long do we protract its life, and so long do we extend the dynamics of imagination. The habit which can perhaps be cultivated is the habit of curiosity, the everlasting desire to learn things unknown. It is here, I fancy, that our education fails.

You have not forgotten those mental tests made with our army recruits when we entered the war. They indicated, you recall, a sky-scraping superiority of the American to the foreign stock. In particular, the Italians were to the Yankees as the subway to the Woolworth Building. Now, although one could not help reverting to the fable of the lion and the man, one was bewildered by the discrepancy between this result and the testimony of Italian arts and Italian schools as compared with our own. To put it bluntly, if we are so all-fired smart, why do our institutions of learning make such a pitiful show beside those of other countries? We try hard enough, and we spend a lot of money on instruction. We brag a great deal, too, about our love of education, though not so much as we did before those same army tests revealed such an astounding proportion of illiterates. The word "education," however, conveys a different idea to the European and to the inhabitant of our United States: to the one it means the university, to the other it means the primary school. When you come to question some of those who talk loudest about the business, you discover that their notion of education is the multiplication table (without undue insistence on the upper part) and the alphabet. Then you begin to ask yourself whether our failure to maintain in the young that intellectual curiosity which is their birthright may be due to aiming too low. Can it be that, all along the line, our instruction is two or three or four years behind the boy's natural development? Can it be that what should be novel and stimulating has lost its kick by the time it reaches him? One reason for such a mistakenly moderate objective would be the parental sentimentality already mentioned. Another would be, in many cases, the ignorance of those who exercise ultimate control, and especially the blindness induced by political and pedagogical oratory. For no one else is so entirely hypnotized by words as the orator.

Let us switch off from education and consider the orator *per se*. Beware of the speaker who begins: "I am not going to make a speech." Among many sad and similar reminiscences, I recall one occasion — a great banquet with several hundred banqueters and a list of about a dozen after-dinner orators, including, I remember, David Walsh and Calvin Coolidge. When coffee had been consumed and the clatter of cups had begun to subside, the toastmaster arose with a smile that sent my heart into my boots, and announced, in a deprecatory tone: "I am not going to make a speech." Save that he said it in Italian, this being an Italian banquet in the banquety days of the Great War: "Io non voglio fare un discorso." At that, one could see all the guests at the speakers' table brace themselves to endure what they knew was to come; and I (for I, too, was on the list) sent a note to the management asking that my discourse be omitted. Such prayers, I have observed, always meet with ready compliance; the only other form of request so promptly and cheerfully granted is an application for leave of absence without pay. Well, after his guileful exordium, the toastmaster went on to state his reasons for not making a speech; they were excellent reasons, and they consumed twenty-five minutes. The next twenty minutes were devoted to a partial enumeration of the things he might have said, had he chosen to make a speech — things which, in the mind of his listeners, fully justified his adverse decision. After that, he proceeded to a consideration of things he would not have said; happily these were not so numerous, and could be disposed of in ten minutes. At the close of his harangue, those speakers who had not succeeded in slyly slipping away were prodded into wakefulness, and their turn began.

Once, and once only in my life, I preached a sermon. I

mean a real, regular sermon in a church, not the informal homily that is so freely bestowed on family and friends. It was a Laymen's Sunday. I cannot flatter myself that I taught the listeners anything, but I learned a great deal. Among other things, I learned why the church clock is placed directly in front of the preacher, and behind the congregation, where the faithful cannot see it without painfully twisting their necks. A deer (happy creature!) can without discomfort turn its head completely backward, holding itself in readiness to gallop away at the first indication of annoyance, whereas an anxious parishioner must either dislocate his neck or shamelessly extricate his watch. I have always sympathized with that lecturer who declared he could bear with the equanimity of long habit a man who pulled out his timepiece and looked at it, but could not endure one who, not satisfied with looking at his watch, would shake it and hold it up to his ear. A clerical friend of mine once told me of the most disconcerting experience he had ever had in the exercise of his functions. An elderly lady of determined aspect, he said, took a seat in a front pew, carrying a little wooden box. When the sermon began, she opened the box, and extracted therefrom an elaborate hearing apparatus, which she arranged, screwed together, and adjusted to her ear. After exactly three minutes, she removed the receiver, unscrewed the mechanism, and packed its component parts snugly away in the box again. And the preacher had to preach on.

I suppose the most copious torrent of eloquence to which I was ever subjected was the speechmaking at the celebration of the 700th anniversary of the University of Naples. I was one of the many delegates — several hundred — from all quarters of the world. It was a glorious affair, with a five days' program of festivities, among them an excursion to Pompei, an all day's sail around the Bay, a gala performance of *La Traviata* in the great theatre of San Carlo. But San Carlo saw another sight on the second morning, the date fixed for the official observance of the solemnity. All over the great stage was ranged the crowd of delegates and political dignitaries. The house was filled with townspeople. In the royal box, opposite the stage, sat the King, who bore himself with the stoical courage he has shown on other trying occasions. On the handsome printed program in an inconspicuous place had stood a request that the representatives of each nation select one of their number as a speaker. There being no indication of when or where the speaker was to speak, I had assumed this notice to be a mere empty formality, and therefore had been considerably taken aback when a little group of my countrymen walked into my hotel at dinner-time, the evening before the ceremony, and informed me that I was it. Protests were vain, and I had yielded, sure that nothing would come of it. But in the darkness of the night I had begun to have misgivings, and, before the arrival of sleep, had concocted in my mind a few phrases that might serve their turn in the unlikely event of their being called for. Lucky, indeed, that I was forearmed! The competition of orators was the most serious part of the whole congress. First came the home team: the Minister of Public Instruction, the Rector Magnificus of the University, the Spokesman of the Faculties, and the Mayor of Naples, all interesting and leaning to mercy's side. Next the foreigners, called off by nationalities, in alphabetical order. In some delegations the election was contested, two or three rival candidates announcing themselves as the people's choice. Such disputes were settled by enforced arbitration. Each speaker, when summoned, advanced to the front of the stage and spoke his piece — or, rather, read it, for all but mine were in manuscript. The compositions were of every length even to the uttermost. Without vainglory, and without danger of contradiction, I can affirm that mine was the shortest. Nearly all of them were in Italian, but a few were in French or in Spanish. Costumes varied from blazingly magnificent academic gowns to plain evening dress and morning street habit. Most conspicuous, for their splendor and for their popularity with the audience, were the South Americans. At the time, my estimate of the number of speechmakers was 150; I shall now reduce that figure to twenty-five, trusting in the rhetorical efficacy of understatement.

The power of litotes was well understood by that guide who had (and perhaps still has) his stand at the entrance of the Louvre museum, an inconspicuous, gentlemanly type, precise in attire, manner, and speech. "Would you like a guide to the Louvre, sir? A guide to show you the pictures?" he would say. "You may have confidence in me. I'm the next-to-best guide to the Louvre, sir." Who would not have confidence? Had he said, "the best guide," everyone would have set him down as a shameless advertiser, probably an impostor; but the "next-to-best" carried a conviction of modest accuracy that was irresistible. I wish our logomachists could go to school to him.

How much depends on the form of appeal! A conscientious colleague of mine, whom for his rigid truthfulness I shall call George, was once standing on the sidewalk in Bowdoin Square, waiting for a car to take him to Cambridge. To a mature Bostonian, even one who does not go back to the halcyon days of Chester Square, these words

convey a savor of long ago. Moreover, it was a horse-car.
Under George's arm, unmistakable to the practised eye,
though disguised in a neat rectangular package, was a
bottle of sherry, which he had purchased at S. S. Pierce's.
Upon him and his burden fell the gaze of a sailorman,
who, after a moment's cogitation, laid his course for
George across the street, and soberly and courteously accosted him. He was a middle-aged man of prepossessing
appearance, fair-faced and blue-eyed, just what the good
sailor in a story-book ought to be. "Excuse me, sir," said
he, with a pleasant intonation; "may I ask a favor of
you?" "Certainly," answered our hero, with the alacrity
of one who does not expect to be asked for money. "Will
you do me the favor of looking me straight in the face
and answering a question truly?" "Yes," George replied,
still promptly, though a bit apprehensive. The modern
mariner held him with his glittering eye. "Do I look like
a drunkard? Would you call me an old soak?" "No,"
said George, considerably relieved at being able to give an
answer at once so veracious and so complimentary; "you
look like a very decent sort of chap." "Now, one more
question, if I may. Do you ever drink?" And still he
looked George in the eye, politely refraining from any indication that he was conscious of the tell-tale package.
"Yes," said George, firmly. "Have you ever by any
chance known what it is to want anything and not to
have the price of it?" Again that uncompromising truthfulness which is the dominant note in George's character
compelled him to answer: "Yes." "Need I say more?"
were the mariner's concluding words. What would you
have answered? So did George.

Such is the power of words, when one is their master
and not their slave!

The Three Bens

B EN JONSON," wrote the schoolboy in his examination, "is one of the three highest mountains in Scotland." Why not the very highest? Presumably the lad, being scarcely sure of his facts, thought it safer to compromise. Always a moderate statement involves less ruinous downfall than an extreme one, if the rider proves to be off the track. "One of the highest" lends itself more readily to plausible justification, even though Ben (which of course can be naught else than a Scottish mountain) be notable only for historical associations. What if Ben Jonson be only the scene of a famous event: may it not be pretty high, just the same? Besides, who ever heard of a Battle of the Jonson, or a Siege of the Jonson, a Diet of Jonson, or a Jonson Convention? Mountains are conspicuous usually for their size, when conspicuous at all; and if Ben Jonson were not conspicuous for something, it would be unfair to ask a question about him. "One of the highest," then. The "three" adds a note of precision, without, if wrong, constituting a bad mistake.

A thoroughly intelligent answer, utilizing all the information possessed by the defendant, and all his powers of ratiocination. A more reckless spirit, bound either to scale the heavens or to fall like Lucifer, would have ventured on "the loftiest peak," perhaps with a touch of lakes and mountains beneath me gleaming misty and wide. This daredevil perchance will some day be a Leader of Men or even a Copper King. Our cautious schoolboy

will never rise so giddily, but will surely develop into a
shrewd and successful man of affairs. Had you, O Reader,
rather be a "perchance" or a "surely"? Your orology
will depend on that. When asked your opinion of the
weather, do you say, "I think it may brighten up in the
course of the afternoon and evening" or "It will be as
clear as a whistle by one o'clock"? Answer me this
question, and I shall tell you whether you are a well-
to-do merchant or a Napoleon of finance — nay, rather,
I should do so, were I, myself, in the Napoleonic class.
Being what I am, I should doubtless call you "one of the
highest," without even hazarding the "three."

In every category there can be only one highest. Let
us, then, learn our place and, resigning ourselves to it,
eventually contemplate it with a proper pride. A picture
in a bygone number of *Punch* portrays an inquisitive
tourist searching a hamlet for its notabilities. Stopping
before a bench whereon is seated an antiquated specimen
of our race, he inquires: "Are you the oldest inhabitant?"
"O no, zur," comes the answer, with a modesty not un-
tinged with self-respect, "I be only the village idiot."
Whatever the community to which we belong, the law of
primogeniture admits of but one eldest; but it is open to
the humblest of us to seek and perhaps to attain the second rank. In fact, I know of at least one candidate whom
I should willingly nominate for that office.

In one of these States of ours lived an ambitious Lieutenant Governor, who, when his year was over, aspired to
a second term. The voters, in illustration of the maxim
that "the majority is always wrong," denied him that
merited reward. Heart-broken by the election returns,
crestfallen, he dragged his slow length along to the un-
desired privacy of his domicile, where he was bravely

greeted by his sympathetic spouse. "Cheer up, Wolsey," she cried. "Never mind the election! You shall always be Lieutenant Governor at home."

"Tell me, Henry," a philosopher asked of his friend, Mr. Peck. "Tell me, does your wife ever get angry if interrupted?" Blue-eyed wonder responded from Mr. Peck's countenance. "Why, how on earth should I know?"

On a ship, as in a home, there can be but one commander. But even in such absolute monarchies as these, the ruler may come to grief by abuse of power. Such, perhaps, is the moral to be deduced from "The Book of the Dun Cow and the Beaver Hat." I say "perhaps" because this is a true story, and true stories, though always a good deal more moral than the stories which people make up, are less likely to lend themselves to a *hæc fabula docet*. I know the tale is true, for it was told me by a sailor. And the sailor was in the ultimate year of his very long life. Of late he had taken to boat-building; I still own the last boat he made — a mighty good boat, too. But I can remember when Captain Ben Jackson was in his prime, a dark, handsome, curly-haired skipper, a great favorite, at our summer resort, with the young people of both sexes (though possibly one was more demonstrative in its appreciation than the other).

In those Arcadian days there were two major sports, buckboarding by land and rowing by sea. Romantic those days were, with moonshine and music on the waters. Youths and maidens loved to swarm out on the ocean at eventide and return after dark. Sometimes the whole bay seemed to be cluttered up with their plashing oars. There were nights when every dip would turn up a glare of phosphorescence; once I saw, with perfect distinctness, far below me, a whole school of mackerel, each individual fish illumined by the glow his passage kindled. But this, you will agree, is getting too pretty to last. Your experience already suspects the thorn on the rose, the fly in the ointment, the skeleton at the feast, the writing on the wall. A danger, a dreadful danger, continually menaced the idyl. Fog. Yes, at any moment a fog, sudden, dense, opaque, might sweep over the landscape, obliterating the points of the compass; and then how were the innocent fauns and nymphs to find their way home? So it came about that Captain Ben Jackson organized himself as a Deus ex Machina. The little flotilla, with its Guidi and Lapi and its Vanne and Lage, instead of scattering itself in perilous profusion, learned under his guidance to proceed in close formation, and, when the mist began to thicken, to trail hard after him, who would row ahead, leading the procession ultimately back to the slip from which it had started. With such a conductor, youth laughed at fog; indeed, it would have been ready with its crossbow to shoot an albatross, had that fowl been there and then extant. In after years, Captain Ben enjoyed telling of these nocturnal expeditions. "And when I finally would get back," he concluded, "they would always ask me whether I had took 'em to the no'thard or the southard o' Gull Island; an' I never told 'em, because I never knoo."

But we are devaricating from the Dun Cow and the Beaver Hat. The yarn really has no point, except as a "slice of life" — the life that was lived hereabouts in the middle of the eighteen hundreds. Here it is, just as it fell reminiscently from the lips of honest Ben Jackson.

"You go roamin' about here quite a good deal, and you may have noticed, way out in the woods near the foot of

Western Mounting, a big heap of sawdust. You can still
see it's sawdust, if you look close, though it's mostly covered with rosberry bushes and looks like a nat'ral mound.
Well, when I was a boy, they used to be a sawmill in thet
place. People in them days used to kerry their mills, with
an engyne, out into the woods where they was cuttin', an'
do their sawin' on the spot. Now, thet mill belonged to
Cap'm Ben Jones, who owned a little medder an' a wood
lot off there in the mountings. Ben Jones, he was master
of a brig that used to vyge out from this harbor. An' between his vyges Cap'm Jones would come an' work his
sawmill an' git in his hay.

"Well, one summer, while him an' his men was runnin'
the mill, they was quite a good deal bothered by a cow —
a sort o' blackish-brown cow — belongin' to Seth Carter,
that used to stray over into Cap'm Jones's land an' eat the
hay an' tromple over everything. They druv her off time
an' time agin, but it did n't do no good; she was always
right back, as frisky as ever. They spoke to Seth about it,
too; but Lord! he was too busy to keer what his cow was
doin', so long as she did n't interfere with his work.

"Well, one day, just before Cap'm Jones was goin' to
sail, there thet cow was, on the rampage agin, an' et up all
the men's lunch. Gosh! how mad they was! Pretty hungry, you know, after a hard mornin' at the mill. 'See
here, boys,' says Ben Jones, 'I'll show you how to fix her,
an' fix her good, so she'll stay fixed an' never hev no call
to come over here no more.' So he told 'em to take a
big bunch o' hay an tie it to her tail an' set fire to it
an' then let her go. Well, they did n't exactly like to do
that. They was pretty mad; but they did n't think it was
treatin' the cow just right. It might spoil her milk; an'
besides, they was afraid Seth might not like it. But Ben

he would n't listen to nothin'. 'Who's cap'm here,' says he. 'Who's cap'm here, I'd like to know.' Them was his words. An' he made 'em do it. He was a pretty rough master, even ashore. Of course the boys wa'n't alto-gether unwillin', neither; they expected to git some fun out of it. An' they did.

"So they got an awful big bunch o' dry hay, an' tied it under her tail, an' teched a match to it. Gosh! you'd ought to seen her. They did n't hef to let her go; she just went. They ain't nothin' could 'a' held her. Fust she let out a beller like a hundred thousand sirene whistles. Really it wa'n't scurcely human. Then she was off like one of them cyclones. Fust she'd run straight for a piece; then she'd go a-whirlin' round an' round, sort o' chasin' her tail. An' everywhere she went, she set fire to every-thing. She burnt up Seth Carter's wood lot, an' Ephraim Harper's, an' Tobias Robinson's, an' Pearl Mayo's, an' Fred Gott's, an' set Archie Conway's barn afire, an' went crashin' through Bill Spurlin's henhouse an' trompled all over his cucumbers. Nex' the Methodis' church went, an' then the Baptis' (but it was a pretty old buildin' an' they hed n't got their noo organ yet). After thet she went a-tearin' through the village, an' it was all they could do to save Alec Sargent's store; an' Rod Fernald's was burnt to a cinder. Then out into the woods agin, an' started the fire that burned over Connor's Mounting an' Hunter's Holler. An' at last she went a-plungin' down into the Lake. An' thet was the last that mortal man ever see of her.

"Well, you know how it is when things gits reported round. They was all sorts o' stories. Afterwards, they was some that claimed all them fires was set by lightnin'. Then they was others said they'd seen a strange man smokin' a pipe out Seal Rock way. Some folks was sure Alec Sargent done it because they wa'n't trade enough for two stores in the village an' he wanted to git red o' Rod Fernald's. Then they was more (specially Methodis') that swore the Baptists started it all, to collect the insurance on their old shack an' buy their noo organ. The Baptis' minister thought it was a visitation o' the Lord, to punish the town (specially the Methodis' part) for its wickedness — though I never could see that our town was much wickeder than some other towns which I might mention but won't. But it really wa'n't none o' them things. It was just thet cussed black-an'-tan cow. Though I can't say 's I blame her very much, either.

"Well, meanwhile Cap'm Ben Jones 'd sailed off in his brig, and did n't know nothin' of all these doin's. It was a beautiful noo brig, an' he was awful proud of her. He was the owner, an' she was all paid for, excep' forty-two dollars that he'd borrowed from old Deacon Rodick. Anybody 'd 'a' ben proud of her. You know what a brig is — one o' them square two-masters they used to hev in the old days? Hahnsome boats, an' able, but they took a lot o' men to handle. She had a fine, square stern that showed up a long ways off. Ben Jones was awful proud of her, an' I can't say 's I blame him very much, either.

"Well, when Cap'm Jones's vyge was over, he come a-sailin' in as peert as could be, an' dropped anchor right here in the harbor. You can see the spot from where you 're standin' now. When evenin' come on, he sort o' slicked himself up an' put on his beaver hat, an' hed two of his men row him ashore, to call on the gals. Thet was his right; he was cap'm. He hed a right to go ashore without leave. An' he hed a right to wear a beaver hat. It was a grand beaver hat, as noo as his boat, an' almost as big. His men they hed n't no shore leave thet night, an' they'd ought to stayed aboard the brig. Whether they did or not, I'll not presoom to say; but wherever they was, they never seen nothin' of a thing that was a-happenin' right there under their noses.

"Well, this is what it was. Just about dusk, a rowboat put out from shore, with two men in it. Folks never could agree about who them two men was. Some said they was Seth Carter and Ephraim Harper; then they was some claimed they was Tobias Robinson an' Pearl Mayo; and others swore they was Fred Gott an' Archie Conway, an' some made out they was Bill Spurlin' an' Rod Fernald. It so happens I know who they was, but I'm not a-goin' to tell. Except I will admit that I was one on 'em. Now one o' them two fellers was a sort of an artist. I mean he could drawr an' paint things a little. An' he hed with him a large can of Asaph's Asphalt Paint. They's a funny thing about Asaph's Asphalt Paint; an' that is, it won't never come off. You can wash it an' scrub it an' scratch it, but there it sticks. Even if you scrape it all off clean, or paint over it, it'll come back agin. Ef you paint a sign with Asaph's Asphalt, the letterin' 'll last longer than the wood it's painted on. Well, them two fellers rowed out quiet in their boat until they come astern of the brig, an' there they moored until the artis' feller'd finished his paintin'. What he done was to paint a great big r'arin' cow, in red asphalt, on the clean noo stern of the brig. Then the two fellers rowed back, as quiet as they come.

"Well, Cap'm Jones he spent the night with some friends ashore. In the mornin', when he come down to the landin', beaver hat an' all, he see quite a crowd o' people a-starin' out at his brig an' a-laughin' fit to split.

The folks was all to leeward of her as she lay at anchor. They was somethin' he never would tell about, but the fact is, he was a little bit near-sighted; an' he was mighty curious to know what was the matter. So he an' two of his gal-friends jumped into a dory and rowed out; an' they hed n't gone fur when he see it all. There was the great red cow a-r'arin' on the stern of his boat. An' when he come closer, he see it was Asaph's Asphalt Paint, that would n't never come off. Even when his brig was all rotted to pieces, thet red cow would still be a-cavortin'. He could scrub an' scrape all his life, but he never would git shet o' thet old cow. An' he would always be reminded o' what he done to her.

"Well, what do you think he done then? I suppose he could n't think o' no right words to say; or perhaps he thought of 'em, but could n't say 'em before them gals. Anyhow, he never let out a peep; but he just took his beautiful beaver hat an' slammed it down ker-slap in the water, with all his might. An' the hat, instead o' floatin' off, just went plumb down like a moorin'. An' that was the last that mortal man ever see of it. An' Cap'm Jones never come back to our harbor agin.

"An' them two fellers that was in the rowboat thet night, they drifted apart as the years went by. An' one on 'em passed away only last winter. An' his restin' place is in Coloradda."

Here Either

THE other day I overheard the following conversation between two young men who, at nine in the morning, were entering their respective offices. "I haven't had any breakfast yet," declared the first. "Here either," the second replied. The meaning of the responsive phrase is immediately evident, despite the mystery which at first aspect veils its birth. "Here either" is manifestly an idiom; that is, a whole which is not equal to the sum of its parts.

Language — real language, distinctive language, colorful language — is almost all made up of idioms. I wonder whether an artificial medium, such as Esperanto, is capable of developing them; if not, it can never take the place of natural tongues, but must remain colorless, purely intellectual. Idioms presuppose a considerable homogeneous group, all ready to take the same illogical short cuts and to make the same incongruous couplings. Until the world shall have faded to a uniform gray, it is scarcely conceivable that such a color-group can exceed the confines of one nation. As a writer approaches the international frame of mind, his style becomes less and less idiomatic; that is, it smacks less and less of locality. Less and less does it evoke pictures of genuine people and genuine places; less and less does it recall to our mental ear the sounds of actual life; less and less does it make our mental nose respond to odors it has really smelt.

And less and less difficulty does it offer the translator. One would not be surprised to discover that ease of translation is a measure of a writer's internationalism; at any rate, of his lack of local attachment. Take Maeterlinck, for instance, who in spirit has dwelt in a world apart, and in body in two countries: if there is any other French prose as easy as his to turn into English (or, I fancy, into any other European language), one would like to know what it is. Yet it is a very beautiful French — limpid, imaginative, logical but not constrained. It is fine French without being peculiarly French; else it could not be so readily transformed into fine English. Try to turn Voltaire or Renan into our language, and his fineness disappears. While the appeal of such as these may be international, their speech is intensely local.

Going back to our suggestive phrase, "here either," we have now had time to analyze it into its two discrepant elements: "Same here" and "I have n't, either." After all, is the expression an idiom — or is it only slang — or is it the thing of one man and one moment, a *hapax legomenon?* Those are three different phenomena; or, looking at it from the point of view of relativity, three phases of the same phenomenon. A chap, whether on purpose or by accident, hits off a new sequence of words or syllables. His creation may, like the Lost Chord, never be repeated; then it stands as an individual performance. If its author be just an ordinary chap, it is forgotten; if, on the other hand, he be a very great chap, his invention ("lego-literary," for example) will be cited forever by those dictionaries which promise their purchasers a larger number of words than any other dictionary; but always with one and the same reference — just as French grammars invariably quote Racine's "la reine, je la suis" to illustrate the use of feminine *la* in place of the usual neuter *le*. Let us suppose, however, that other people are so tickled by our chap's happy thought that they use it themselves and pass it on to still others. It becomes current in a certain *coterie*, perhaps in all sorts of *coteries* that affect a jocose or a slipshod tone: then it is slang. For slang, as you know, there are special lexicons, which have to be renewed every year or two. If, now, our stranger holds its own, and achieves adoption by graver people in their graver moments, it is a full-fledged idiom, and has its *entrée* in all dictionaries as well as in volumes contrived especially for its housing. It has become a part, and an essential part, of a language. Although most of our idioms were born ages ago, too long ago to be traced to their childhood, new ones are coming into the world with every generation.

A considerable part of the vocabulary of slang, before it either perishes or achieves respectability as idiom, is more or less narrowly local. Some of it may belong to a particular college, a single camp, to a quarter, a town, a state. But in this country, at least, it seldom remains long thus circumscribed. If it is good for anything, it is quickly spread by newspapers and theatrical performances, and comes to be recognized, even if not readily used, throughout the length and breadth of our land. Such diffusion, however, does not assure immortality. Who under forty, nowadays, would understand "Like a hen," which was on all lips forty or fifty years ago? Like oblivion, I doubt not (and I say it without sorrow), awaits "So's your old man."

Once I heard a lecture by the historian, John Fiske, wherein he pictured the colossal wastefulness of nature. The peaceful grove, the green pasture, the still waters are the scene of incessant fierce and pitiless contest which inevitably results in the extermination of the vast majority of the contestants. One tree survives at the expense of scores of other trees and shrubs, weed kills weed, fish gulps down fish with a comprehensiveness that passes belief. Consider the innumerable offspring required by plants, insects, fishes, in order to keep the species extant. "A single salmon," declared the teacher, "produces in one season twenty thousand young. Think of that, children: twenty thousand—a single salmon!" "Teacher!" cried the inquiring little Evelyn. "How many young does a married salmon produce?"

Similarly it fares with phrases, legitimate and illegitimate. Most of them perish, though not in such tragic proportion as bereaves the salmon family. They are begotten by thousands and survive by tens. Creatures of fashion, they depend on the whims of that fickle goddess. Until yesterday, we could not stand an outrage; today we will not "stand for" it. Of late we have cultivated a love of superfluous adverbial tags, much the sort of thing that in German is called a "separable prefix." One matter "connects up" with another, a thug "beats up" his enemy, the victor "wins out." A student writes in an examination: "At about this time they was a conflict between Classicism and Romanticism, and Romanticism one out." As yet, to be sure, we do not "out-win," but we may come to it; then we shall be quite Germanized. I once heard a Yankee child of three, judging that his younger brother's bedtime had arrived, advise his mother: "Mamma, dress baby un." But he was ahead of his age.

At the present moment the Britishers (especially Oxford, perhaps) have developed an amusing fad of trying to pronounce English words according to the quantity of the vowels of the Latin originals from which they came, quite regardless of the fact that "long" and "short," as these terms are currently used in our tongue, designate qualities as remote from ancient Roman usage as China from Peru. When the aforesaid mode was in its infancy, an American Latinist who was in close touch with this new Oxford Movement expressed a certain measure of dissent from the rigorous application of the rule, which, he contended, would lead to some unexpected and preposterous results. "But," he concluded, "there is in my mind no doubt that in cases where the Latin had a diphthong, *æ* or *œ*, we must use long *e* in English. Hence we should say 'ēconomics' and not 'ĕconomics,' because the Latin here had an *œ*, representing, as you know, Greek *oi*." "Do you speak as a peedagog?" I inquired. "Great Scott!" he ejaculated, in his dismay forgetting to employ a more distinctively British exclamation. "Do you know, I always thought of that word as having something to do with feet!" He is not alone. Many people not devoid of classical training interpret an orthopedist as a man who straightens crooked feet — as, in fact, he often does.

Slang being to some extent local, as I have said, one easily confuses it with dialect. Properly they are quite distinct, although in the rough and tumble of practical use it is hard to keep them apart. Dialect should mean a type of English (or of some other language) which has developed out of the parent stock side by side with the speech which has come to be regarded as the standard. If you go back far enough, the offshoots are so different that they are called separate languages, as for instance Danish, Dutch, English, and German, all from primitive Germanic. Going not quite so high upstream, you get such variations as Yorkshire and Kentish, which are English but not standard English; these are dialects. In our country, real dialects, in this sense, hardly exist, because a central standard had been developed and considerably generalized before our people came over here. The different kinds of speech which we call "dialects" are in the main outgrowths of the general standard type. We are very prone, however, to apply the word to a local slang vocabulary; still more frequently we use it of English mispronounced and otherwise mishandled by foreigners in our midst. The "German dialect" comedian was long, and perhaps is yet, a favorite figure on our stage; and scarcely less familiar was the "German dialect" writer. Of course the phrase "German dialect" should designate Saxon, Bavarian, or something of that sort; we, however, mean by it simply English unintentionally Germanized. Thus it comes to pass that Chimmie Fadden, representing the slang-ridden usage of the East Side, and Hans Breitmann, exemplar of the English spoken by our German-born citizens, share with the Hoosier Poet the use of the name "dialect" for the lingo they employ.

By some it is affirmed that British usage and American usage have split so far asunder that the two variations merit not only the designation of "dialects" but the more grandiose title of "languages." Witness Mr. Mencken's amazing book, *The American Language* — amazing in its interest, in the extraordinary acumen, observation, and industry it exhibits; amazing, too, in the wide favor it has won among readers generally unused to so grave intellectual pabulum. I should not agree with the author in his postulate that British and American have reached a stage of differentiation comparable to that which distinguishes, for example, Spanish from Italian. Indeed, I suspect that if a scholar of equal parts should undertake an equally exhaustive examination of the peculiarities of the two old commonwealths of Virginia and Massachusetts, he might register an almost equally valid claim for a "Massachusetts language" and a "Virginia language." But perhaps I am wrong. Surely I am right, however, in contesting Mr. Mencken's attribution of all the glory (or all the blame) for the bifurcation to cis-Atlantic ingenuity. Sometimes it seems to me that stolid John Bull has moved faster and further than spry Uncle Sam. It would be an interesting experiment to take, say, a year of the *Spectator* and compare it, on the one hand, with a recent year of *Punch* and, on the other, with the same year of *Life*, listing the innovations in vocabulary and idiom, and thus furnishing a basis for determining which has deviated the more from the real Addisonian. I think I know what the answer would be; but I am not going to tell.

Is it harder for a Yankee to read *Punch* or for a Britisher to read *Life?* As someone has said, each man thinks his own task the hardest: the farmer has to talk dialect and the humorist has to spell it. A great part of the difficulty encountered by our two suppositious readers, however, lies not so much in the dialect itself as in the strangeness of the topics which the respective dialects discuss. On one side of the ocean you have cricket, horse-racing, and fox-hunting; on the other, baseball, business, and bootlegging. When shall the twain meet? To an appreciable extent they have met, though, already, in the common interest of war; doughboy and Tommy can now communicate without an interpreter.

The upshot of it all is, I do not believe the race for modernity has been a walk-over, with poor old Britain left

alone at the post; at worst, it has been neck and neck, like
the race between the two undertakers. What was the
race between the two undertakers? Listen, my children,
and you shall hear. Two funerals were wending their
solemn way to Mt. Auburn Cemetery, the one proceeding
along Mt. Auburn St., the other along Brattle, which two
streets come together (as all the world knows) shortly before the graveyard is reached. At this point the driver of
hearse No. 1, becoming aware of the approach of a rival,
gives a little flick (oh! just the tiniest flick) to his horse.
Seeing which, the Jehu of hearse No. 2 bestows upon his
animal a somewhat smarter smack. Automedon the First
swings the whip with a freer hand. Jehu the Second
lashes out with the spirit of the race-course. On and on
rush the two chariots; one would have said the Circus
Maximus, or Barnum and Bailey, or the thrilling scene in
Ben Hur. Erect on their flying vehicles stand the two
contestants, plying their gory whips; foam bathes the
flanks of the plunging steeds, blood trickles from their
nostrils. Wayfarers huddle together in fright on the side-
walks. The two funeral processions come straggling after,
as best they can. Close and frenzied would have been the
betting, had there been any betters or any time to bet.
Just at the gateway Automedon forges ahead, beating
Jehu by a full length. "Wall," cries the victor, trium-
phant (in private life he is Silas Peck), "wall, I beat ye,
did n't I, Ben (for Jehu is not Jehu's real name)?" "Yaas,
ye did, Silas," admits Ben-Jehu; "but," he adds, with a
significant glance at the winning hearse, "but *I*'ve got
my corpse with me."

Of the antiquity of this story a philological commenta-
tor could give three proofs. Firstly, he has heard it before
(and he does not hear very many); secondly, the Silas

Peck, alias Automedon, of the narrative contents himself
with saying "I beat ye," without expanding it into "I
beat ye tew it," as he would have done at any time within
the last ten years; thirdly, the very plot of the tale carries
it back to the paleo-hippic age, when hearses were drawn
by horses. Yes, jokes, like books, have their fates; like
idioms, their vicissitudes. In the dear old days before the
war, the Germans had one jest which they never failed to
tell you. Picture to yourself a merry little social gathering. Perhaps there is a bit of music; but that is not
requisite for the development, although it helps considerably. Presently your jovial hosts begin to hitch un-
easily in their chairs, and anxiously to scan your facial
topography, to see whether the propitious moment has
arrived. Then one of them, as it were the high priest of
the rite, clears his throat and speaks: "When we Germans are particularly happy, then we always sing 'Ich
weiss nicht was soll es bedeuten, dass ich so traurig bin.'"
And the other celebrants roar with glee until the tears
roll down their cheeks. Will those Arcadian days ever
return?

We Americans are more disposed to tragedy. According to the *Harvard Graduates' Magazine's* account of the
Commencement afternoon exercises in a recent year,
"proceedings were brought to a close by the singing of
Fair Harvard by the Alumni Chorus." How potent is
song! What matters it who writes our Constitutional
Amendments? But we must not stray from our subject.
I was saying that deep in the hearts of my countrymen
the tragic spirit prevails. Whereas the Germans profess
sadness in the maddest of their merry-making, we profess
gladness when our souls are in the lowest depth of misery
— I mean, when we are making an after-dinner speech.

We, the honored guests, always begin by declaring at unconscionable length how excruciatingly happy we are to be present; and all the while our only-too-truthful faces are registering naught but unalloyed gloom. To be sure, there is always the unanswerable question, who suffers more, the speaker or the listener. What token shall tell us? Can gloom be gauged? Can misery be metered? "I am saddest when I sing," cried Keats Hemans Dexter, the Sophomore. "No!" firmly rejoined his room-mate. "*I* am."

"That is an old joke, too," says the man who always wants his money back. What do I care? The book out of which I got it is a good book — *The Evening Entertainer, or One Thousand and One Merry Jests,* published at 23 Chestnut St., Philadelphia, in 1813. All stories and all pleasantries can be traced back and back and back (else there would be no science of Comparative Literature) until we reach their ultimate source in Adam. It was he who invented them all. He had a fruitful mind. He invented language. He is the author of Original Sin. "Say, Ad," sighed Eve, "I have n't tasted that apple yet." "Here either," replied our First Progenitor.

Cruising in 1924

RELATIVITY. We always vaguely knew it, but could not formulate it until Einstein came and gave us the word. For in human creations the word is generally at the end, not in the beginning. So it must be with finite resources. First, little by little, more or less by accident, the achievement, then the definition. Already from our successive experiences with our two feet, with the horse, with the bicycle, with the automobile, with the aeroplane, we unconsciously apprehended the fluidity of our concepts of space and time. Now, having the word, we can talk about it. We realize that space and time are a matter of velocity.

I suppose most of my fellow-countrymen flatter themselves they know what velocity is. In this land of rapid living, where there are more automobiles than in all the rest of the world, — one, it is said, for every five inhabitants, man, woman, or child, with accidents to match, — in these machine-packed United States, one might be justified in assuming that the *ne plus ultra* of speeding had been attained. That is, the assumption would be justified *a priori*. It is a perfectly good assumption, as long as one confines one's observations to the home field. But it falls, as soon as competition is admitted. Talk not of fastness, O my countrymen, until ye shall have beheld the Portuguese (of the Argentines and the Greeks I cannot tell), until ye shall have shot breathless through the narrow streets of Lisbon, annihilating space and time — and, by some miracle, annihilating naught else, save your national illusions. There shall be seen two machines, plunging head-on, directly at each other, heedless as two mad suns careering through ether, yet at the last moment dodging, impelled by some mysterious impulse to opposite sides, missing each other by an inch, and coursing away unperturbed. It all seems very astronomical — or atomical, as you choose; it helps you to understand the strange conduct of electrons. There shall sharp corners be turned, without slowing and without skidding, and, to your amazement, without smashing the house opposite. All this, too, unassisted by "the influence of liquor," which seems to be an absolute requisite of any comparable swiftness in our country. Let us hang our heads.

But our humiliation is not yet complete. As the American scorcher is but a turtle to the Portuguese taxi-driver, so is the Lisbonite but cold molasses to the Arab. When, in a crazy old Ford, held together by catchpins and shoestrings, ye shall have dashed and bounced and flown, taking all the many curves on two wheels, from Jerusalem to Bethlehem, or down to Jericho (it really is down — over three thousand feet), or twisted and spiraled about the squirming, climbing alleys of the town under the star, scattering donkeys, driving humanity into doorways, striking terror into the heart of the ordinarily supercilious camel — when this experience shall be yours, then may ye speak understandingly of speed. Then shall ye know how a streak of jagged lightning feels — if lightning, in its jagged state, has sense enough to appreciate its perils.

Somehow, the wildness of your flight accords with the wildness of the country. Until I saw it, I never imagined anything so savage, so barren, so utterly forbidding — bare, dusty mountain after bare, dusty mountain; dead, windswept terraces of rock; habitations that are but holes in the cliff, a soil producing a perennial crop of stones, which cover it as completely as a pavement covers a street. Small wonder that the favorite sport of the natives should have been stoning people to death. Small wonder that a fisher should have been nicknamed Cephas, which is Rock. Yet for the painter this landscape is full of fascination — all delicate, soothing tints of rose and yellow, especially when the day is far spent. Indeed, in the spots where the hard top has been removed, — on the laboriously constructed terraces, perhaps four feet high and two feet deep, — the earth appears to be fertile, even up in the hills. Along the shore is a strip of good black dirt, which is now coming under cultivation at the hands of hard-working Orientals, begowned and beturbaned, who look like Arabs.

But in discoursing of drivers, we must not let the East blind us to Naples. Indeed, many things in Naples are suggestive of the Orient; notably the continual low-pitched, monotonous "a-a-ah," wherewith a driver stimulates his steed. The Arab coachman or carter, however, is kind to his horse, whereas the best that can be said of the Neapolitan is that he is not so cruel as he used to be. He has, however, much to try his temper. His public vehicles are the oldest, shabbiest, decrepitest, fleafullest that ever rattled and banged and quaked and creaked and miraculously held together. His pavements are awful beyond belief. One would attribute them to ancient Roman days, were not those in Pompei so much better. And this in a country where all the other cities are beautifully paved. It would seem that whenever a Neapolitan wants a dozen stones to repair his house, he simply digs them out of the street, leaving a chasm a yard square.

At the sides of the road most of the cobbles are worn out. So it is all the way from Pompei to Baia. One consequence is that streets are impassable save in tortuous streaks, and a driver's main business is to get into the channel before a driver coming from the opposite side can reach it. How they avoid collision, I never could quite determine; I suppose, at the last moment, one fellow's nerve gives out and he swerves. It is most exciting, of course, when the two rivals are automobiles.

Recently, I had an admirable chauffeur, who took me to Cava and Salerno and Pesto and Amalfi (the first day after the route was re-opened) and Sorrento. His artistry in taking sharp curves, especially in spots where the parapet was gone and nothing intervened between the edge of the road and five hundred feet below, proclaimed him a superman. Yet he had one fault, a fierce hatred of horse-vehicles, which he evidently regarded as an odious anachronism. Whenever he saw one, he would go for it, like a terrier after a cat. That so many escaped destruction is eloquent testimony to the alertness and agility of their drivers. After all, perhaps, the Neapolitan coachman should not be too harshly judged if he occasionally lambastes his horse and always sets his meter at "night tariff" for a daylight fare.

It is not thus in Cairo. The Arab coachman is generally content with the incessant, gentle "a-a-ah," which, when I first heard it, I took for a Moslem prayer; he carries beside him an immense bunch of fresh, luscious fodder, and he sees that his beast gets a plenty, whether business suffers or not. The carter is in the habit of walking beside the cart, to lessen his animal's burden. Sometimes, to be sure, one sees, in a funeral, a dozen black-clad, closely veiled women squatting on a flat cart drawn by one little donkey; but the donkey trots merrily along, apparently unaware that he is overladen; and the male mourners walk. A similar indifference is shown by the haughty camel, as he stalks majestic with two cartloads of building stone swung in two bags over his mighty back.

A camel's back, by the way, is not such a bad substitute for a Pullman chair as one might imagine, although the kneel and the rise are at first a bit surprising. Once started, the motion is a comfortable rhythmic swing, except when the stiltlike creature speeds up. As to donkeys, the ease which they afford is common knowledge, even among the inexperienced. Still greater luxury is secured by the expert (be he Oriental or Neapolitan), who sits very far aft.

Fond memories come back to me of Columbia, the donkey who conveyed me from Bedrashen, up the Nile, through ancient Memphis, with its palm grove, its colossus, and its beautiful Sphinx — such a contrast to the famous but dilapidated relative beside the Great Pyramid — to the tombs and pyramids beyond. It was a long ride, and might have been wearisome, but for the conversation of my donkey-driver, Abdul, who footed it beside us. Abdul was a past-middle-age person *sans* most of his teeth, a poor man, he assured me, who had never been to school and could not read, the parent of numerous children, frequent appealers for bread when he could offer them nothing but the comforts of religion. Indeed, as we traversed a village, he pointed out to me several of the most conspicuous in a swarm of juvenile backsheesh-hunters, and claimed them as his. Yet his discourse, in the main, was cheerful, even gay. "Ah, it was a happy day for Abdul when his Father came to visit him in the desert!" "Blessed the boat that brought Abdul's good

Father to him!" "My Father is a kind, generous Father, and Abdul has no fear." Gradually it dawned upon me that the Father in question was not our Father in Heaven, but no other than my innocent self. At this manifestation of relativity I draw the line.

From time to time my Abdul would affectionately stroke me on the back, and he constantly did his best to make the journey not only instructive, but entertaining. When Columbia brayed, he would shriek with laughter, crying "Music, music!" To my inquiry about a curious black-and-white bird, common in Egypt, he answered, with another peal of merriment: "It isn't a bird, it's a crow," pronouncing "crow," Cockney-fashion, to rime with "cow." Snatches of American and English soldier songs he frequently quoted for my delectation.

As we approached our journey's end, however, I noticed a cloud of anxiety. Ever more fervent in his assertion of my parenthood, more fervent still became his faith in my bounty. "I know my Father will not forget me," he cried again and again. "Tonight my poor children will eat, and Abdul will remember his kind Father in his prayers." More than once I had to soothe him. At last the moment of separation came, as come it always must. Have you ever seen a famished dog expectantly watching his master at table? That was Abdul. Who could have had the heart to disappoint him? Dipping into my pocket, I produced a fistful of small coin; and I was about to dip again, when, holding up his hand in protest, he exclaimed: "Stop, my Father! It is enough."

Abdul is not the only Egyptian who has won a friendly niche in my memory. Pleasantly do I remember Soliman, tall, broad, masterful, with a big bass voice, an easy control of his long gown, a smile half friendly, half mocking, on his handsome face. Several times my dragoman, he never asked for anything and was invariably content with the little I gave, yet always seemed eager to accompany me again. He was by nature a scholar; every summer, in the wonderful museum, he took a course in Egyptian archeology. I am just a wee doubtful about his ornithology; for he gave the name of "vulture" to the omnipresent and intriguing black and white bird which Abdul, with more plausibility, called a "crow." But in archeology he was not only expert, but critical. After showing us the tree under which the Virgin Mary rested, and narrating the story, he added: "Such is the Christian tradition. But should you consult the Koran" (and he cited chapter and verse), "you would find that in truth the tree under which she sat was not a sycamore, but a palm." This he apparently communicated to satisfy his own conscience, without much hope that it would penetrate. His attitude toward the outlander, as nearly as I could fathom it, was one of amused contempt. Yet he was anything but a blind fanatic — slyly skeptical in matters of religious formalism, scornful of the obligation of wearing slippers over one's shoes in a mosque; and he never betrayed us into the hands of shop-keepers.

I wonder who buys all the European-manufactured stuff one sees for sale in the bazaars. Really, there seems to be no enforcement of the law of supply and demand. But perhaps I am mistaken. In Constantinople our compatriots will buy ridiculous little canes, which no man, however stout of heart, would dare to carry in his home town; still less would he dare to give one to anybody. An elderly companion of mine, stout of heart and stout of girth, got four of them at one swoop, and for days afterward chuckled with delight over his astuteness in obtain-

ing four for a quarter, instead of three, the dealer's original offer.

The American quarter passes as currency pretty well
around the Mediterranean shore, though not in Egypt,
which is trying to exclude all foreign coin, the Egyptian
pound being worth a little more than the British. But
the great desideratum is the American paper dollar.
Every inhabitant, from Madeira to Palestine, seems to
have accumulated at least one dollar in United States
quarters, and is eager to exchange it for a bill. I must
have made half-a-dozen such transactions in Funchal
alone. It appears that United States paper enjoys a pre-
mium over the silver which it is supposed to represent.
Why, I cannot say, being no economist. But in this operation, which brings gain to one participant and no loss
to the other, I was happy to note an ideal application of
economic law.

The land of the Nile I saw at a perfervid moment —
politically, I mean, not thermometrically, although the
mercury, too, was well up. It was the opening of the
first Egyptian parliament, and the cry of "Egypt for
the Egyptians" was at its loudest. Speaking of cries, I
noticed that those of the crowds, when they were not in
Arabic or some other Eastern tongue incomprehensible
to me, were in French; none were in English. "Vive le
Roi!" I heard repeatedly; and sundry other favorites
were invited to live, in the language of Paris. I was well
placed to hear, for my hotel, the Continental, was the
centre of festivities. One evening a banquet was given
there to the King, General Allenby, and two hundred
deputies. The beautifully illumined park and opera
house were just opposite my balcony; the square in front
was the chief gathering place. There was no disorder and

no foolishness; but evidently there was deep-seated enthusiasm. It was rather pathetic to see a people so delighted over the acquisition of a Congress.

Italy also I watched at a critical time, the election season. There everything was as quiet as the grave. In Pisa
just before the day, and in Florence on the day itself, nobody appeared excited; but the squares were full of men
softly conversing in little groups. In posters, and in the
press as I saw it, only one side was represented. While the
voting went on, the *carabinieri* carried guns strapped to
their backs; and through the streets, here and there, hurried black-shirted boys with loaded canes.

The same uncanny calm seemed to reign in Constantinople, in the days just preceding the deposition of the
Sultan. Everything appeared to be going on as usual, the
huge city was busy and well kept, in spite of daily changes
of regulations; but there certainly was an atmosphere of
repression, of distrust. Our ship was continually overrun
with officials and with civilians, as it had been in no other
port. There seemed to be not only inspectors, but spies,
and spies on the spies. Our own officers were evidently
apprehensive while we were there, and greatly relieved
when we got off without trouble. In the city, young men
of the aristocracy were organized to offer their services as
amateur guides. Their leader, a vivacious cosmopolitan,
with Chesterfieldian manners and a perfect command of
both French and English, was an interesting host. My
conductor, for one day, was the grandson of a famous
Turkish general, whose portrait he showed me in the mili-
tary museum. This youth, a student of agriculture, had
spent his boyhood in France and spoke French almost like
a native. While I was lunching at a hotel, he brought in
and introduced to me a Turk of considerable eminence

both in education and in international sports — a handsome, alert gentleman of fifty, who spoke fluent French
but no English. The newcomer was extremely eager to
make a good impression on Americans, to help them to
correct their erroneous views concerning the young government. "They really know nothing about us," he said,
"they have no understanding of the things we are trying
to do." He was even contemplating a propagandist tour
in the United States, and was beginning to study English
for that purpose.

In fact, we do know little enough about Turkey. Until
this year, I never suspected that the mosque, at its best,
is a very close rival to the grandest Gothic cathedrals; nor
was I aware that the great museum of Constantinople
contains the finest examples of high-relief sculpture in the
world — the so-called "Tomb of Alexander" and that
other tomb known as "The Weeping Women"; nor had I
any idea how superbly picturesque a corner of ancient
city walls could be.

Well, the Turks have not done much to ingratiate
themselves. Of late, they have been ridding themselves
of outlanders; especially, they have been dismissing or
freezing out their foreign employees — much to the disgust of an old German pilot, with whom I had a whispered
talk on board ship. They could not well discharge him, as
they had dropped the others, he declared, because, having
served here for thirty years, he was known as the only
competent pilot for his special route; but they had cut off
nine-tenths of his salary. He was now living on his sav-
ings, but could not keep it up much longer, as he had a
son in a German university and a daughter in some school
in Constantinople. What to do when his capital should be
exhausted, he did not know.

While we were lying off the Golden Horn, there arrived a steamer full of Russian refugees, so closely packed, apparently, that they could not sit down. They were not allowed to land. What became of them, I could never learn; it was reported that they meant next to try the Holy Land. "Turkey for the Turks" was the motto, even as "Egypt for the Egyptians."

Among the people I met in Egypt was a Nile dragoman, richly attired, stately and austere in bearing, who spoke English better than most of his fellows, with a decidedly British accent. He was, however, as he told me, a Bedouin from Algeria. On the Nile boat, an American lady tactfully asked him how much he would take for his silk scarf, which was, indeed, very beautiful. "My clothing is not for sale," he answered. "But," she insisted, "how can you afford to wear such expensive things?" "You must not suppose," said he, "that every dragoman is poor. This scarf was my father's and my grandfather's. I shall pass it on to my son and my grandson." Presently, as we passed some carcase-looking object in the water, and the passengers were idly speculating about it, a facetious compatriot of mine turned to the Bedouin and remarked: "It's a dead Arab." "It is not a dead Arab," was all the dragoman answered; but I would not have given much for the life of the joker, if the two had been alone in the desert. There was much merry *badinage*, too, about departed kings and dynasties. Finally the Bedouin took me aside and said: "If you and your family will pick out a few more persons who are really interested in Egyptian antiquities, I shall be glad to accompany you. But I will not guide a crowd of empty-headed, chattering, giggling Americans, who know nothing and want to know nothing and make a silly joke of everything."

There are all kinds of conductors. There was the smiling but not always reliable Moses. There was the venerable Ali, who courteously began all his statements with the phrase, "You know very well that . . ." (and not a tinge of irony). Then there was young Mohammed, easy, dapper, sophisticated, sly, whom we engaged to protect us from human pests, and enable us to enjoy in peace a short excursion, including a second visit to the pyramids near Cairo. This valuable service he rendered with skill. On the other hand, he soon showed a disposition to steer us into sideshows which were not on our program. When my wife remonstrated, pointing out to him that it was his business to save us from bother, not to bother us himself, he exclaimed sadly: "The lady hates me with hard words!" But he took the hint. On the whole, he did pretty well for us during the day, and extremely well for himself when it came to the settlement.

One of our guides in Jerusalem interested me, a round, diminutive man with dachshund legs, who seemed to be of Turkish stock. In religion, however, he was a devout Roman Catholic, profoundly contemptuous of the errors of the Greek church. He had several daughters in a French convent school, and by his ecclesiastical affiliations was able to let us into some things which otherwise we should not have seen. He was, indeed, determined that we should see everything. Well posted he was, full of spirit, untiring in his trot over the horribly wearisome cobblestones. His jacket was sadly spotted and he had a huge rent in his little baggy trousers. This I understood when I heard some passers-by address him respectfully as "Professor." The acquaintances in question were Italians, and his Italian greeting to them solved a problem of communication. For his English was by no means ade-

quate to the volume of information he had to impart; and
I was therefore relieved to find that he spoke Italian like a
Tuscan born. French, too, he handled with the greatest
ease, as I presently discovered. To my inquiry how he
came by these languages he replied that he learned them
at school in Jerusalem; and on my expressing some surprise (though by no means all I felt), he outlined to me his
high-school course in science, history, and linguistics, and
finally carried me off my feet with an outpour of Latin.
Sometimes I wonder whether American education is all
that it is cracked up to be.

It may be comforting to turn to a less educated guide.
At Taormina an agreeable youth offered to show me
about, in the west end of the place. In this most charming of towns everything old that is not Greek or Roman is
Saracen. Saracen the ancient walls, Saracen the ruined
fortress perched high above (where in early days, my conductor said, "the Saracen cannon used to go boom,
boom!"), Saracen the falling Badia, Saracen the basement of the ducal Palazzo. My young man was particularly impressed with the antiquity of this last building,
and did his best to impress it on me. "Old, old, very old,"
he kept saying. "When was it built?" I finally asked.
After a moment's hesitation, he answered: "Prima . . .
prima di Dio" — "before God."

I like a guide who is full of enthusiasm, of local spirit.
Perhaps the most enthusiastic I ever met was a native
Athenian. I shall long remember his tall, gaunt form
erect on the windy Acropolis, his piercing eye, his pene-
trating voice, his intense desire to bring home to his
listeners the glory of his city, his despair at any mark of
inattention. Beside the Nile, too, I found no end of pride
in the bewildering remoteness of the dawn of Egyptian

civilization. "You talk of Rome, of Greece," said one dragoman. "What did Greece or Rome ever possess that she did not first get from Egypt? What good thing is there in the whole world that was not first Egyptian? Egypt is the source of all the culture of the earth." In smaller things, also, there may be vainglory. Long ago, the sexton of a Protestant church in Paris was showing me, with severe satisfaction, the fine features of the building. "A very pretty church," said I. Looking about him with a loving smile which Calvinism could not quite repress, "Elle est coquette," he admitted.

No, pride is not always proportionate to its object. Having a little time to spend, one day, in Monaco, I hired an automobile to take my family about the place for two hours. The chauffeur was a friendly, intelligent lad of eighteen or twenty. He drove us conscientiously through every street and every bit of road in the Principality; he had no license to go outside. Then he passed through all the streets again in the opposite direction. Finally, at the close of an hour and a half, he confessed himself at the end of his resources, and we settled the charge on a three-quarters basis. During all our drive, however, he never tired of singing the praises of his minute fatherland. "It is a little place, of course," he said, "but what has the bigness of a country to do with the happiness of its inhabitants? What the people want is tranquillity, the chance to pursue their business and their pleasure without interruption. That is what we have here: absolute security of life and property. Nowhere else is traffic so well regulated. Nowhere else are streets so clean and unobstructed. Nowhere else is police protection so perfect. You can walk in any quarter by day or night, carrying all your money, without the slightest apprehension. There are no strikes, no disturbances of any kind. Everybody is satisfied. That is what counts — tranquillity. When you consider what it is that really matters, there is no country equal to the Principality of Monaco."

If you should tire of heat and fashion in Monaco, and should want to go straight back into the Middle Ages, near the sky, amidst a gorgeous mountain setting, tear yourself away from the Casino, and take the funicular road from Monte Carlo to Turbie, at the top of the upper Corniche. That, in itself, is one of the most thrilling and least costly expeditions open to an ordinary mortal; and at the summit, looking down on sea and shore, is a hotel, the Righi, where board is fabulously cheap. But do not stop there yet. For on the road, as you leave the train, is a fiercely whiskered and gentle-spoken man with an automobile, who will offer to take you for a drive. He has three trips, all described in plain lettering, with the prices, on his machine. Moreover, he has an excellent map, which he will gladly discuss with you, being an enthusiast on topography and mountain landscape. His French is a bit queer, but offers no real difficulty. One of his roads goes to the east, one to the north, one to the west. If you cannot take all, choose the middle one, which is newly opened — indeed, not quite finished, and, between bank on one side and precipice on the other, not wide enough for two vehicles to pass, except in three or four spots. If you are so fortunate as not to encounter another car, this route will bring you, after an hour or so of scenery that takes your breath away, to the little village of Peille.

There is one modern thing in Peille, a conspicuous and rather pretentious monument to the young men of the place who were killed in the late war. Perched on a little peak that juts up from the gorge, it seems to represent the

twentieth century intruding on the thirteenth. The village itself, a conglomerate mass of changeless dwellings, is
packed into a space no bigger than Washington Square.
There are no streets, only tortuous little alleys — both
sides easily reached by one's extended hands — clamber-
ing and diving, now steps, now bridges, now tunnels, one
over another, pell mell. I doubt whether the oldest inhabitant can ever tell exactly where he is going; yet even
the novice cannot fail to emerge somewhere, although of
course he can never take the same route twice. Above
climb the mountain tops; below sweeps a ravine, expanding into a great valley, towards Nice.

At the end of the automobile road, outside the village
and somewhat higher, is the old church with its old
tower and with vestiges of the little old fortified monastery. As you enter, you hear a sound of infantile treble
alternating with an authoritative male voice. The priest
is instructing the children of Peille — perhaps a score of
them, pretty tots, who stare at you with greedy astonish-
ment. A hopeful light, too, begins to shine from their
eyes, and their hope is presently justified; for, despite
your protests, the hospitable *curé* dismisses his class, not
altogether unwillingly, one suspects, and to the manifest
exultation of the flock — which nevertheless lingers near.
Then he proceeds, in a businesslike way, to show you the
church. He is a small, slight, lively man, versed in archeology, critical (indeed, rather skeptical) in his chronological estimates. Some things, however, undoubtedly
are Merovingian, notably a rude stone font. Much that
has been attributed to an early date belongs to modern
times — that is, to the twelfth and thirteenth centuries.

The machine can carry you, nowadays, very far back.
It can take you in comfort to places formerly reached only

by the stoutest hardihood. From Monte Carlo, from
Nice, from Cannes, motors and motorbusses can show
you in a day what used to consume a week of strenuous
travel. So it is in Italy. You can get a car with a route
and a chauffeur in any of the principal cities. Florence is
a good starting-point. You can have one-day outings to
Vallombrosa amid the pines on the heights, where once
in May I got caught in a terrific snowstorm; to ancient
Certaldo, Boccaccio's birthplace, sitting on its hill; to
that higher hill where nests San Gimignano, the city of
medieval towers; to Ravenna; to Prato; to Pistoia. Or
you can extend your journey to several days. That is
what we did; and I look back at it as the prettiest journey
I ever took.

The weather was fair, after much rain. It was an April
country, full of flowers, with all the dainty tints that
seem so unreal to eyes accustomed to the downright hues
of a dry atmosphere. We had a good closed car (for it was
still cold) and, as chauffeur, an adroit young Florentine.
Most of the journey was a novelty to him, a great romance. How his eyes would sparkle with excitement and
admiration! He had a small road-map, which he kept beside him on the seat, and every now and then he would
stop and inquire the way. Occasionally we went a little
awry and had to turn back; but that only heightened the
sense of adventure.

Our first halt was at Siena, well known to me from bygone days, and happily unchanged in all essentials. New
to me, however, was the great stretch of bad lands —
gullied clay-hills, gray and buff, with scant vegetation —
which we traversed the next day, faring eastward. New
to me, yes; but strangely familiar, too, from the back-
grounds of early Tuscan pictures. Towards midday the

countryside became more smiling; hill-towns appeared, clinging to their perches. At one point, a vast and beautiful expanse of water unfolded itself; the driver looked at me inquiringly. "Trasimeno!" I shouted; and he beamed with delight. We followed Trasimeno around, clambered into the mountains, and finally went honking up the great hill of Perugia, our second objective. There we found quarters spacious and cheap — everything but comfortable, for the best hotel was completely filled with well-to-do German travelers; but what did it matter? We were in Perugia. Which is the loveliest of the Italian hill cities? When you are there, the answer is easy: it is the one you happen to be in. Far away, in retrospect, I think I should accord the palm to Perugia. Surely there can be no other view quite so exquisite as the outlook from that little terrace above the cathedral. With such a landscape before him, who would not be a Perugino?

From Perugia to Assisi the sacred, where beauty enshrines hallowed memory, and hallowed memory enhances beauty. No other spot is altogether so moving — not even Jerusalem.

Then to Orvieto. The road, most of the way, runs on the top of a mountain ridge, and one gazes into an infinity of faint rose and gold and tender green. How fond one becomes of faithful old Mont' Ammiata, which meets one at Siena, and day after day looms in the offing! Orvieto itself is as original as the flavor of its wine, secure on its high plateau encircled by precipice. Nothing else is quite like its gorgeous cathedral. Nothing at all resembles that strange, deep well, with its double spiral staircase running around it to the bottom.

From Orvieto to Rome, you are mostly on high land, but you go down and down. Montefiascone you pass, not unrefreshed. You pass Lake Bolsena and Lake Bracciano. You pass Mt. Soracte. Once in the great city, you have to tell the driver how to go, for he was never there before. He is somewhat embarrassed, too, by having to turn to the left, whereas in Florence and on the road one then turned to the right; but he quickly adjusts himself. An exciting search awaits us. It is Holy Week, and Rome is crammed with Italians and with foreigners — the latter being mostly German. The hotel to which we had written cannot receive us; nor can another, nor the next three others, as we drive desperately to and fro in the deepening dusk. At last, happy refuge! we are accepted by the dearest hotel in town, the Excelsior, which can offer us its dearest suite. But it is well worth the price, which, after all, translated into dollars, would be moderate in New York. Our chauffeur leaves us, with a sympathetic sigh of relief; and our excursion is over.

Our car and driver we got from a most convenient national society known as the Movimento Forestieri. Its Florence office is next to your bank, on the Via Strozzi. One can get an outfit also at Cook's or at the American Express Co., but it costs nearly half as much again. Cook's of course is the oldest agency, and the most popular. When I was a little boy, I once met in England the original Thomas Cook. I remember him as a short, genial man, with a face tanned to the color of an Indian and still further darkened by a frame of white sidewhiskers. It was his boast that he had visited all the countries of the globe and still spoke no language but his own. In spite of all temptations to belong to other nations, he had remained an Englishman.

Thos. Cook & Son's is not what it used to be. There was a day when it offered the traveler economy as well as ease and security. Now it caters to the opulent; and, where it once held the field alone, it has several competitors. There are times, however, when one must resort to the old firm. I needed its help to visit Sicily. The island was packed from end to end with wealthy German tourists: it was hopeless to attempt a trip unless every bit of accommodation was secured long in advance; and only a great organization like Cook's could get and hold the reservations. Every hotel had to be telegraphed to, and a specific promise received by the office, before a schedule could be made out.

Our party was to leave Naples at midnight by sleeper and, at the close of the tour, return by steamer from Palermo. Everything went well up to the last stage — whereof I shall speak presently. Proper night service is a new thing in Europe, but now it is considerably better than ours, if two persons are traveling together. Sleeping-cars are furnished by an international company. A single polyglot expert unites the functions of conductor and porter; instead of an indeterminate gratuity, he receives (in Italy, at least) a fixed fee — one-tenth of the price of the ticket — for which he gives bill and receipt. The car, except for a corridor running along one side, is divided into small two-berth staterooms, very narrow, but most ingeniously provided with every conceivable comfort; and the cost scarcely exceeds that of an ordinary section in one of our promiscuous Pullmans.

The general abolition of tips in Italy has relieved travel of its most burdensome annoyance. Today, guides and taxicab drivers are the only people who expect them, although some café waiters and some museum custodians are willing to pocket an affront. In hotels, however, and in dining-cars, there is on the bill a regular ten per cent

charge for service, and that is all. An extraordinary trans-
formation, brought about, I am told, by the waiters themselves. Certainly the service is even better than it was;
never before have I seen the whole staff of a great hotel
so self-respecting and at the same time so beaming with
courteous and hospitable alacrity. I regret to say that
swarms of vulgar American and German profiteers are
doing their best to destroy this paradise. Among the un-
organized classes not included in general anti-tip agree-
ment, there is now hesitation, though no longer assurance
of a gratuity. At the top of Vesuvius, the simple old
guardian who had taken us around remarked ere parting:
"This is a beautiful day, sir. Many days are rainy or
cloudy. Those are bad days. Then the strangers who
come here are disappointed; they cannot see anything,
they are cross, and they give nothing to the guides. This
is a beautiful day, sir." But let us return to our tipless
Sicilian passage.

Our train crossed the Strait of Messina on a ferry. The
return journey from Palermo to Naples, however, requires a night on a tolerably big steamer. There it was
that the hitch came. I had been advised by Cook's to see
its Palermo agent as early as possible, in order to make
sure of my reservations. That warning I heeded; I sought
Signor R. two days in advance. To my dismay, he expressed grave doubt whether accommodations could be
had. The new administration, he said, had just established a rule prohibiting, on all government-owned trains
and boats, any reservation of places until the day of departure. That, it seems, was a fact, although some miti-
gation is possible in practice; for instance, a big concern
like Cook's can often obtain, on the day before, the
promise of a reserved seat or room, though not the seat or

room ticket itself. I suspected the agent of having sold me out to some German millionaire (a not infrequent occurrence among hotel-keepers), and I made a protest of appropriate dimensions. Mr. R. then suggested that I try my hotel porter, who, he declared, had several berths assigned him for distribution. But the porter, while admitting that he had control of some sleeping-quarters (I have resisted the temptation to say "berth-control"), vowed that, inasmuch as I had Cook's ticket, Cook's agent was bound to provide for me. Again I sought the agent, who again sought the steamship office; but to no purpose. Enormous crowds were going on every steamer. Apparently there was nothing to do except wait for the day of sailing, get up at four, go to the navigation office at five, and stand there in line until ten, when the wicket would be opened (it was open but two hours, from ten to twelve) — only to be told, in all probability, that nothing was left. It looked like spending the rest of my life in Palermo. Palermo is an interesting place; but I had seen it pretty thoroughly, and the mosquito season had begun with great gusto. Besides, I had to be in Naples in two days, having been appointed Harvard delegate to the great celebration of the seven-hundredth anniversary of the University of that city.

In this extremity, I had myself conducted to the sanctum of a very great man, the head of the Sicilian passenger department, whose quarters were near the railway station. He was a youngish man, tall, elegant, sedate — just one's idea of an Old World diplomat. His first utterance, on hearing my plea, was a repetition of the agent's verdict: I should have to take my chances with the others; such was the law. Then it was that I bestrode my tall steed. I was not an ordinary passenger; I was the official representative of the oldest and most famous university in the United States to the greatest university of Europe; I had been invited by the University of Naples, whose authorities had already greeted me and assigned me a place; my absence would create comment; I was, in a sense, a guest of the State. The statesmanlike director meditated for a moment on this aspect of the case; then nodded, and wrote some message in pencil on a sheet of paper, which he handed, with a few words of instruction, to his secretary of legation. The dapper secretary thereupon accompanied me to the railway station, into the bureau of the chief of the ticket department, to whom my tale was unfolded anew. This official, a plain, businesslike man, after inspecting the communication from his superior, told me all would be well, and, there being four in my party, male and female, picked out for me a big four-berth room, the best he had. The ticket, however, could not be delivered now. I must present myself on the morrow (the day of sailing) at ten — not at the passenger wicket, but at the *freight* wicket — and call for him. You can guess how promptly I was at the designated spot. There, after several delays, I got the attention of the chief. In due time this officer called me around to the passenger wicket, and gave directions to the ticket-seller, from whose hands I obtained at last the precious document. Had I not been able to make myself understood in Italian, or had I not been fortuitously a delegate to Naples, I should at this moment have been a permanent citizen of Palermo. When I related my success to the hotel porter, he asked: "How much did you have to give him?" My reply that I gave nothing but words was received with a polite smile of incredulity.

Our gallant ship, when it sailed that evening, was so

full that its sides seemed to bulge. Most of the passengers were Palermo students, on their way to attend the Naples festivities. They were attractive lads, but dreadfully noisy for the first hour, after which Neptune obligingly claimed tribute from the greater part of them. Poor chaps! No quarters had been assigned them; they passed the night lying all over the decks and in the life-boats. Perhaps, though, after all, they were better off than we favorites of fortune who had berths; for our berths swarmed with hungry bugs, and our door, which had no lock, was opened from time to time during the night by sociable or inquisitive fellow-travelers.

The Naples festivity itself, grandly conceived and grandly executed, would make an interesting story in itself. But it is another one; to introduce it here would mar the unity of this narrative. Suffice it to say that the reform movement has hit the town hard, and made it (save for its pavements) in very truth a New City.

Many years ago I took my family to Pompei. We had had a pretty irritating experience in Naples. There were three small children in the party, and it was impossible to mobilize quickly when beggars and fakirs attacked. We were an easy mark. In Pompei it was worse; for here the imposition was all organized. To begin with, the big board, just inside the entrance, stating the legal tariff for all the sights, had been carefully scraped so that the figures were illegible. Then, your particular guide, instead of showing you the whole show, as he was expected and paid to do, turned you over in every street to a special street conductor, who in turn betrayed you at every house into the hands of a house custodian, who passed you on to the keepers of the several rooms and closets; and all these useless people clamored for compensation.

Then there were sellers of pictures and ornaments and relics, and umbrella lenders if it looked rainy, and sunshade lenders if it was too sunny, and friends and relatives of the various guides and vendors, and plain undisguised mendicants, and retainers of the mendicants, so thick that one could scarcely see the ruins, and so loud that conversation was impossible. On the way back to Naples, in the crowded train, I related something of my trials to another visitor who was standing next me in the aisle. He was a German, I remember, but for some reason we were talking French. I noticed that a gentleman seated near by seemed to be listening. When, at the next station, a good many passengers had got out, he beckoned me to sit beside him in a place just vacated; then he begged me to repeat to him in Italian the tale of grievance I had just unfolded. Willingly enough I did so. "I am very glad," he said, "to have had this chance to get accurate information; it is so hard for us to know the truth. The Government is most anxious to suppress the abuses you describe, but I suspected they were still going on. It is nearly impossible to introduce reforms in a population banded together and for centuries accustomed to live on extortion. I am going to ask a favor of you: namely, that you put your story in writing, with date and signature, and send it to me. Such testimony will have great weight with the administration. I am the Director of Excavations." And he gave me his name and address. He evidently meant business, for things improved marvelously, I was told, in the following years. Even now, although there has been some relapse, they are vastly better than they used to be.

Always one used to meet a good sprinkling of German travelers in Italy, but they were not over numerous (ex-

cept in Venice, long the Niagara Falls of newly wedded
Teutons), and they were generally agreeable companions.
But now a new race has sprung up — a race of German
profiteers — and precipitated itself upon the peninsula.
Clamoring for the best accommodations, smoking the
costliest cigars, drinking champagne at all their meals,
pushing and elbowing everywhere, they are quite as ob-
noxious as any of the Americans of Martin Chuzzlewit
days; and they are every bit as vulgar. Most of them
give the impression of folk who have never traveled before and have no inkling of civilized usages. Their re-
semblance to hippopotami would be perfect, if the hippo-
potamus were a devotee of the toothpick.

The most amazing thing about them is their number.
When I was in Italy last spring, it was impossible to believe that anybody was left in Germany; the whole population seemed to have moved down into Ausonia. In the
streets of Florence one heard more German than Italian.
Naples and Sicily were absolutely Teuton. A visitor from
Mars would have called the phenomenon a new racial mi-
gration, caused, not by poverty at home, but by excess of
wealth. Little by little, these overfed invaders came to
be known as the "starving babies." One simple-minded
Yankee after another would say to me: "Here I've been
denying myself and my family, to feed these people's
children. Never again!"

For the crushed and jostled tourist, however, there is
occasional solace. Picture an excursion steamer, loaded
with five hundred people (mostly Germans), setting out
from Naples to visit Capri. On arrival, the ship, of
course, has to lie three hours or so off the Blue Grotto,
while the sightseers, in boatloads of two or three, visit
the curious interior. Then, after two o'clock, a starving

crowd is conveyed to the nearby town and there transferred again to rowboats, in order to land for luncheon.
These skiffs hold six or eight apiece, and the rush for them
almost capsizes the ship — a prelude to the coming play.

O tu che leggi, udirai nuovo ludo!

Late, very late, when nearly all the passengers are disposed of, a few Americans venture to approach the steps,
hoping to find a place in one of the last boats. Vain hope!
They are unceremoniously thrust aside, and the seats
are filled with human hippopotami of the most hippopo-
tamious variety; and off they go. As the food-hunters
come alongside the shore-wall, in some thirty feet of
water, they voraciously jump up, shoving one another,
each trying to beat his companions to the eating-house.
In their mad haste they all climb on the gunwale. Over
goes the boat, and splash into the sea goes every climber.
Such a swashing and sputtering and shrieking never
gladdened the ears of Capri before. One by one they are
rescued. There really is no danger, for they float like
balloons. But one particularly rotund and vociferous
hippopotama (if I may so describe her) long eluded sal-
vage. Hands would seize her, arms would strain; little
by little she would be warped in, agonizingly hoisted,
brought almost to the edge; then she would slip; plump!
she would go bellowing into the billow, and the process
would begin afresh. It was half an hour before the hali-
but was landed. And meanwhile the first arrivals were
busily gobbling up all the comestibles on the island.

After all, though, the plight of this unfortunate female
could not fail to stir a note of sympathy in the heart of a
Luxury Cruiser; it was so like the landings of a Luxury
Cruise. On board ship the life really is all luxury; so is

most of the hotel life ashore. But between ship and shore there is a dreadful hiatus, over which it were best to draw a veil. "If this be luxury," cried one sufferer, "give me the simple life!"

My own chilliest experience was at Athens. I may say, in passing, that nowhere else in the world have I seen so many boats together. In fact, they were wadded in so tight that I could not see how any could ever get out. Well, we landed in a high wind, many of us wet; but we had a glorious day. For our return, we were warned to be on the dock at Phaleron at five. And there we were, shivering in an icy blast. Presently, as many of us as possible were stowed aboard a transport, where we sat or stood, unable to move, exposed to the gale, wondering when (or whether) we should start. This lasted four hours. Always colder, always more threatening; rumor after rumor circulating among the congealed disconsolate; but no departure. At last came a report more plausible than the others, and more hopeful: our boat was to put out as far as it safely could and was to meet a larger transport, which, after we should have been shifted to it, was to convey us to the steamer. And so it eventually happened. At nine or so, we really did move off, slowly and cautiously. After a long interval of frozen gloom, our spirits feebly flickered at sight of the second transport, big as a Rockland steamer. Long, long was the transfer. Then an everlasting silent voyage through the darkness until the lights of our own vessel were descried. Rocking and swaying we came alongside. One futile attempt followed another to make connection. Deck after deck was tried. Several passengers were taken very ill, and one man fainted. At last a gangplank was laid from the very top deck of the tossing transport to Deck C of the great

liner. Poles held at each end by officers served as railing.
But the ships kept drifting apart, and, as the passengers
were rushed across one by one, a gap would appear between the transport and the gangplank. Luckily no one
fell through. By half past eleven we were all safely and
thankfully on board, warming ourselves with warm sup-
per, and vowing never to risk another landing party. But
of course we did.

At Madeira we had luck, better luck than we appreciated at the time. At Lisbon, Gibraltar, Algiers, Constantinople, we lay not far out, and the shore service was
pretty good. Cadiz was bothersome because of the awful
waits; there was only one transport, and it had other
duties. Landing at Haifa was a lengthy process but not
particularly unpleasant; and the long climb by rail up to
Jerusalem was interesting enough to atone for its discomfort. So Jerusalem itself made amends for wet sheets in
a cold, damp cell of a bedroom in the French hospice.
Naples and Alexandria were the prize places; there we
could lie alongside a wharf. The everlasting bore at
Alexandria was waiting for the customs, and then rushing
through a mob of raucous Arabs to get seats in the train
for Cairo.

I have reserved Tunis for the end. That was the place
that nearly spoiled our schedule. We anchored about
seven miles out, and were ferried ashore in fairly still
water. The city, as you doubtless know, is at the inland
end of an oval bay, a great salt-water pool, nearly land-
locked, largely artificial. The real sea and Tunis are connected by a narrow-gauge railway. According to our plan
we were to spend two days in the city, going out each
night, however, to the far-distant ship to sleep. This was
a hazardous project, and its execution would have been

most comfortless under the best conditions, with half an hour of rail and seven miles of transport by sea in the dark.

During the first day a fierce gale arose, a pertinacious, uncompromising gale. When, at evening, we arrived, shivering, on the bleak outer shore, we were told that no boat could reach the ship. On the other hand, new arrivals from the city declared it was impossible to get accommodations there, several cruises having arrived simultaneously. Many passengers nevertheless went back; many lingered in the dark and cold, hoping a ferry would venture out after all. In fact, at midnight, a craft did risk it, and succeeded in carrying a lot of forlorn humanity to the ship. These we saw no more, as long as the vessel remained off Tunis; for nothing would tempt them ashore again.

My own little party, as night was approaching, with no hope in sight either at sea or on shore, adopted a desperate remedy. Finding that the little narrow-gauge road ran on beside the coast to Carthage, and ascertaining that a train was due ere long, we took a leap into the dark. Dark indeed it was when we reached the Punic city. Far up the hill, where the lights burned, was a hotel; so the station-master assured us. We plodded upwards, steering by the lights. These belonged, as we ultimately discovered, to a large building, which we took for the hotel. A monastery it turned out to be in reality, as we learned from an Arab who opportunely emerged from obscurity. He led us, however, to the goal of our desire, which was not far off.

What a relief it was to find a French inn, modest and clean and ridiculously inexpensive, and a French landlady almost as glad to receive us (her only guests) as we were to be received! From our balcony we could look down, far away, on the lights of our ship. Sunrise revealed an unforgettable view; and the scant remains of Carthage occupied us, in wind and shower, until noon, when we took train for Tunis.

It blew hard all that day, and there was no communication with the steamer. We, however, having had time to investigate, found a wonderfully gay restaurant, the "Chianti," and a sedate lodging-house, where we spent the night.

The third day was still windy; and the sad crowd which gathered on the outer shore did not know whether transit could be made. After endless suspense, a boat did venture forth; then another; then another. All eventually reached their destination; but there were exciting moments — one, particularly, when a transport caught the top of her mast in a lifeboat davit on the ship.

Such is life on a Luxury Cruise. Was it worth while? Did the romance, the sense of adventure, make up for the pain and peril of stormy landings? Did the irritation, the wearisome waiting in line, outweigh the many happy hours? Was the expense justified by the opportunity to see wonderful places to which individual initiative would never have sufficed to take us? It is all a question of relativity.

Myths

HOW often we say: "I hope this story is true!" And we try to believe it is, although we know that so very few anecdotes are. Maupassant somewhere develops the thesis that national history, as children learn it, is made up of silly yarns about kings, preferably their mythical utterances. Any prominent figure serves as a magnet to attract floating tales: witness Abraham Lincoln in our country. The safest way is to disbelieve them all — which, of course, need not prevent one from repeating them.

A story has its own life to live, generally a long life, from age to age; but its existence is as dim and faint as the afterlife of the Homeric Greeks, unless it can attach itself in each generation to some specific character of that generation's acquaintance. It becomes, then, a sort of vampire, sucking life-blood from one full-blooded man after another, lest it fade once more into a ragged, bony, hairy wraith. Boccaccio's most plausible tales are those which deal with Calandrino or Guido Cavalcanti, not those which chronicle the adventures of "a certain merchant."

"A certain gentleman, who was a lover of fruit trees, having observed one morning, to his profound chagrin, that his arboreal favorite, a beautiful cherry-tree, had been felled since his last inspection, summoned his youthful son, a lad renowned for his veracity, and inquired of him who had done this evil deed." That might have done for a Latin composition book, but it never could have prospered without such protection. The Æsopic "certain woman" who "nourished a bird" (as we used to translate it), although the bird in question laid a golden egg, is poor indeed compared with the egg which Christopher Columbus did not lay, but stood on end.

In general, the more conspicuous the person, the wider the currency of the anecdote among the masses of mankind. Some stories, however, content themselves, for the time being, with a restricted *clientèle*, even with a family circle. It is always something of a shock to discover, in an ancient joke-book or a collection of fables, some incident that you had unquestioningly attached to your Uncle Hiram. Uncle Hiram must ever after remain a diminished figure, most of his vitality having been absorbed by the now discredited vampire. At times this greedy creature, not satisfied with one victim, feeds on several at once. One Monday, in Baltimore, I heard a very witty repartee attributed, with all manner of appropriate detail, to Professor Gildersleeve; and the following Wednesday, in New York, Gildersleeve became Brander Matthews, with no loss of minute particularity. Either of these gentlemen, I am sure, might have said the clever thing in question, but I am even surer that neither would have copied it from the other, and I am surer still (if there be three degrees of sureness) that they did not both devise it independently. From shattered faith one recoils to absolute skepticism. I do not believe either of them said it. It probably goes back to Douglas Jerrold or Sheridan or Joe Miller.

One has the privilege, at times, of seeing a myth in the making. The myth I now have in mind has to do with another professor, a mythful but by no means mythical celebrity whom I shall disguise under the name of X. One afternoon a colleague of his, a member of his own department, said to me: "Have you heard what happened to Professor X this morning?" And he proceeded to tell an amusing tale, specifying the classroom and the hour. It was obvious that he firmly believed what he was relating. On the morrow, the story greeted me from every quarter, and in a few days it was all over the college. It will undoubtedly find a place in the learned professor's biography. A bit later, I met X himself. "Do you know the yarn they are telling about you and Y?" I asked. "Yes," he replied; "it's very funny." "Is there any truth in it?" "Not a particle. It is made up out of whole cloth." And he is a painfully veracious man.

Instead of the false yarn, here is a story about him that is really true. He and I and a few others were at a club, about to take tea at his invitation. Having given his order with great precision to the colored attendant, he added impressively: "And bring it with celerity!" The negro scratched his head, hesitated a moment, then brightened up and departed. We waited. Then we waited some more. Then more yet. Finally, with the desired tea, the cup-bearer appeared, his face beaming: "Ah got 'em," he cried triumphantly. "Dey wa'n't none in de house, but we sen' faw 'em. We sen' way to de market; an' ah got 'em!" On the tray was a great bunch of celery.

I suppose that of the anecdotes current, one in a thousand may be correctly told and applied. The foregoing is that one. A true story has no other value than its intrinsic value as a story, its attachment to the protagonist being entirely the work of fortune; while the mendacious ones, or those falsely assigned, reveal, by their very attribution, something of people's estimate of the person to

whom they are affixed. They are a "human document."
Anybody's "celerity" might have been syncopated into
"celery"; whereas the popular myth of Professor X could
never have flourished with any other hero. The cherry-
tree incident might have happened to Aaron Burr or
Benedict Arnold; but it would then have meant nothing,
and would soon have been forgotten or at least transferred to somebody else. But the fact that it was pinned
to the Father of his Country (no matter when, how, or by
whom it was invented) bears witness to the esteem in
which his countrymen have held him who has been first in
their hearts. It follows that of the personal paragraphs
which make up most of our traditional history, only the
true ones are historically unimportant. We have also
gained a criterion by which to judge the veracity of such
tales: if the story is quite out of accord with our general
conception of the character, it is likely enough to be a
real happening; if, on the other hand, it is in harmony, the
presumption is that it is a fake.

The essentials of history are not the things that occur,
but the things that are thought to have occurred. The ex-
plosion of the magazines of the Maine, in Havana Harbor
in 1898, was in itself a regrettable but insignificant mis-
hap; but the conviction that the Spaniards blew up the
ship brought on the Spanish War and the entry of the
United States into World Politics. Similarly the immediate cause of the World War was a belief that Serbia had
been guilty of the murder of a couple of Austrians.

It is the 99 per cent fiction that makes history so interesting; when it is reduced (as well-meaning people are
nowadays trying to reduce it) to the one per cent fact, it
loses all its charm and most of its importance. The price
of eggs in Xenia, Ohio, in the autumn of 1878, does not

quicken my pulses at all, nor does the knowledge of it contribute one bit to my payment of the present cost of the fruit of the hen. On the other hand, the preservation of that arch-romancer, Captain John Smith, by that silly fool of a Pocahontas, has stirred my blood and created in my mind an ineradicable prejudice against the Indian race.

Some people build mausoleums for themselves while they are alive. Others do it figuratively by constructing their own myths and providing the same with their signature. Captain Smith is an example; another is Dr. Cook. It is, however, possible (though hard, I confess) to tell a plain, unvarnished record of one's own experiences. The very difficulty of the task is a spur. Here goes for a try.

On the way from Boston to Cambridge, after a soporific evening devoted to inspection of ill-ventilated municipal night classes for adults: such is the situation. Scene, an electric car, in the not so ancient days when electric propulsion was still a novelty. Imprudently I read the *Transcript*. Increased drowsiness. May have nodded a little; not sure. Of a sudden, the tram stops; I start up. Must be Harvard Square. Yawn. Only two passengers left, myself and a strange man. Dark outside, and raining. I have an umbrella; the elderly stranger has none. With the prompt courtesy so characteristic of our hero, I offer him a share of mine, and we sally forth. He seems to be a stranger not only to me, but to the place as well; for he asks distrustfully: "Is this the way to Brattle Street?" I reassure him; but, ere long, things look very peculiar even to me. I do not rub my eyes, because I am holding the umbrella, but I try to furbish my intellectual vision. There is a church, indeed, across the way, but if it is the familiar First Parish in Cambridge, it has curiously changed since morning. Abruptly a light dawns on me. I recognize that sawed-off stone tower. The Brattle St. for which we are headed is not the Cambridge Brattle St., but Brattle St., Arlington. I have been carried four miles beyond my destination. Looking behind me, I see the car just slipping away on its return journey; and I know this is its last trip for the night. It is no time for ceremony. Without a word I leave the Old Man of Menotomy planted in the rain, full of amazement at this incursion of mystery into his menotomous existence, and sprint for the car. Being, in those not so ancient days, an agile sprinter, I overtake the fugitive and sink, breathless and alone, into a seat. Presently the conductor enters, more (I suspect) from professional than from purely social motives; but he pauses and looks at me wonderingly. "Was n't you in this car comin' out?" he inquires. "Yes," I admit; "but I dozed and was carried past my street." "That's too bad," he sympathizes. "I generally make a point o' tryin' to wake up them kind o' people."

Benjamin Franklin The Reformer

THE world moves fast and it moves slow. While the mechanics of life are transformed with bewildering speed, many of its fundamental problems stay just the same. A couple of years ago Mr. Punch announced: "It is said that the government will soon be broadcasting intelligence by radio"; and added the still pertinent inquiry, "where will the government get it?" But though intelligence may for untold ages be a rare commodity, there is never lack of information. In the words of a character in Freytag's famous old play, *The Journalists:* "So many things happen, and so awfully many things don't happen, that a conscientious newspaperman need never lack copy." Now already these happening and not happening things, happily or haplessly, are being wafted by wireless to a waiting world.

Among the things that happen may be classed scientific discovery, scientific fact, scientific guessing — much of it fascinating to the listening public, if aptly presented. To utilize this great reservoir of curiosity for the outpouring of scientific truth, the International Research Council (so I read) has been concerning itself with the organization of the radio medium. How can it most effectively be done? The question is a live one in England, and perhaps here. A standardized speech is found to be one of the first requisites — an identical English vocabulary and a single

type of English pronunciation; there is demand even for
something of wider application, for a universal broadcasting language. A general auxiliary means of communication — such as Esperanto — has for years been a
desideratum for international science and the object of a
quest by the Research Council. Shall there be also a general wireless language for the whole earth? If so, shall it
be a made-up lingo, or shall it be one of the great tongues
that the nations have slowly developed? In the latter
case which shall it be? That is the ticklish question.
Local jealousy aside, everything points to the choice of
English, not only because of its wide diffusion, its com-
posite vocabulary, its almost total lack of inflections, but
also because this country of ours is the world's broadcasting center, as it is the center of the moving-picture
industry. These two great influences, radio and the cine-
matograph, are now added to the conspicuous advantages already enjoyed by English in the race for linguistic
supremacy.

To win the contest, however, our language must hold
together and must be rid of encumbrance. In point of
fact, it does hold together surprisingly well. Considering
the vast territory, under different flags, where our tongue
is used, the differences in usage are slight indeed. In oral
speech there are, to be sure, deviations from uniformity,
most of them good because they afford the spice of variety; while spelling, on the other hand, is virtually uniform, and uniformly bad. Bad, that is, from the point
of view of the racer for universal favor. It is probably
the worst-spelled language in Europe, the most heavily
burdened with heterogeneous absurdities; and a com-
petitor needs all lightness to win the game. This has all
been talked out before, again and again. The only point

in now bringing up the subject is that we seem to be, whether we like it or not, on the brink of an era of standardization; and if we must be standardized, willy-nilly, we should see to it that the impending revolution in our orthography, which is sure to be involved in the process, be as wisely directed as things can be which are caught in the whirl of revolution.

An unexpected acceleration has overtaken the fluctuating, slow, scarcely perceptible progress of English orthographic change. A potent new cause has been added to the always existing reasons for reform. Only a dead language can have a petrified shell. As long as speech is alive, it develops, like the chambered nautilus, and clamors for remodeling of its chambers. If growth of the integument is arrested and halting, expansion is likely to come in bursts, violent in proportion to the duration of immobility. The revolutionary leaders may be poets, ever sensitive to the attunement of sound and shape; they may be scholars, filled with scientific disgust at the patent falsehoods which our spelling tells; they may be hard-headed practical men, eager to eliminate waste, intent upon a maximum of linguistic efficiency. All three have in England collaborated in a mammoth petition to the government to appoint a commission to study the subject of spelling and spelling reform.

To the last of the three classes — albeit he had a poet's vision and a scholar's clarity — belonged that sturdy philosopher who, parted from his native Boston, chose for his home the city of brotherly love. How much of our distinctive modernity we owe to him! Lightning-rod, telegraph, telephone, radio itself — in all this he had a hand. He invented bifocal glasses. There is no end to his inventiveness. He invented a scheme of spelling reform.

Written in 1768, his little treatise, *A Scheme for a New Alphabet and Reformed Mode of Spelling; with Remarks and Examples*, did not see the light until after his death. We must look for it in the complete edition of his works, by Jared Sparks, Boston, 1840, where it is to be found in volume VI, at page 295. Had it appeared in his lifetime, it might have influenced the progress of education, as his electrical experiments contributed their bit to the swift onward march of physics.

This work of the master is only a sketch, never wrought out to the finality which closer and long-continued reflection might have given it. Precious it is, however, for more than one reason. In the first place, it furnishes us with a key to Franklin's own pronunciation, a specimen of the cultivated American usage of the middle of the eighteenth century. Whether Boston or Philadelphia was the more responsible for his practice, we cannot tell, the standards of the two cities being at that time so nearly alike. Secondly, it adds to the accumulated verdict of the aforesaid poets and scholars and men of affairs the emphatic vote of one of the most practical human beings that ever lived. Can spelling reform be the fanciful dream its opponents imagine, if it commends itself not only to a Milton and a Tennyson, but to a Franklin? Lastly, his project indicates the fundamental cause of our orthographic chaos — to wit, the inadequacy of our alphabet to represent the multitudinous sounds which we exchange; and it suggests the one really curative treatment, the adoption of new letters.

Of the twenty-six characters used by him, six are of his own devising; a rather awkward combination of *o* and *a*, to represent both the *a* of *ball* and the *o* of *folly*, which the author evidently felt to be identical; a sign resembling an italic *y*, standing for the neutral vowel of unaccented final *er*, for the "short *u*" of *unto*, and for the long vowel of *learn*; a symbol remotely resembling a written *h*, to suggest the consonant which we write *sh*, as in *ship*; an *n* with a loop at the end, meaning the *ng* of *among*; two different modifications of *h*, to signify the two sounds of *th*, as in *think* and in *thy*. On the other hand, *c*, *j*, *q*, *x*, *w*, and *y* are discarded. "In this alphabet," Franklin says, "*c* is omitted as unnecessary; *k* supplying its hard sound, and *s* the soft; *k* also supplies well the place of *q*, and, with an *s* added, the place of *x*; *q* and *x* are therefore omitted. The vowel *u*, being sounded as *oo*, makes the *w* unnecessary. The *y*, where used simply, is supplied by *i*, and, where as a diphthong, by two vowels; that letter is therefore omitted as useless. The jod *j* is also omitted." To convey the sound of *j* in "James, January, giant, gentle," Franklin combines *d* with his symbol for *sh*. By substituting *t* for *d*, he gets a notation for "the sound of *ch*, as in *cherry*, *chip*." The initial sound of French *jamais* (which we have, of course, in such words as *vision*) he writes *z* plus his *sh* symbol.

It will be seen that he leaves the alphabet, as he found it, with twenty-six letters, his six new ones taking the place of the six he throws away. Obviously the number is insufficient, and the inevitable result is that some sounds generally distinguished, though more or less similar, are here confounded: for instance, the vowels of *ball* and *folly* (as already noted); the vowels of *fool* and *full*; the vowels of *hut* and *heard* and the neutral vowel used in the unstressed syllables of *about* and *sofa*; the vowel *u* and the consonant *w*, the vowel *i* and the consonant *y*; the second element in the consonant groups of *itch* and *edge*. These are not very serious flaws in a "broad" system; they do not even argue defective hearing, since they may be due merely to expediency. On the other hand, Franklin has the great merit of devising a symbol for a group of newly developed vowels which had hitherto gone unrecorded — the vowels of *hut*, *heard*, and *about*. The failure to distinguish completely *sh*, as in *pressure*, from *zh*, as in *measure*, is curious. Indeed, there is nothing to show that our philosopher appreciated the difference between surds and sonants. He writes *s*, not *z*, at the end of *runs*, *refines*, *degrees*, *shines*, but *z* in *grows*, *shows*. Nor have we any evidence that he recognized the nasal resonance in *m*, *n*, and *ng*. He did, however, understand the relation of "long *a*" to "short *e*" and of "long *e*" to "short *i*"; the accented vowel of *remained* he noted by doubling the *e* of *mend* (or else by using a circumflex accent over it); the vowel of *deed* by doubling the *i* of *did*. One would have expected him to adopt a like method for the vowels of *fool* and of *full;* but in point of fact he does not distinguish them at all.

Concerning the physical production of vowels, his few observations are of no account whatever, unless we are to infer from them that his *o* has very little rounding. With regard to consonants, he noted accurately the factors that come naturally within range of the eye. For example, he describes the *th* sounds as "formed by the tip of the tongue applied to the ends or edges of the upper teeth," *s* "is formed by the breath passing *between* the moist end of the *tongue* and the *upper teeth*"; *r* has "the top of the tongue a little loose or separate from the roof of the mouth, and vibrating."

What do we learn, from the author's brief exposition of his plan, and the three phonetic texts which accompany it, about his own pronunciation? In the first place, we

may infer that the long vowels, of *road* and *made*, for instance, were pure monophthongs; the diphthongal utterance of them seems to have developed early in the nine-
teenth century. Next, and most important, is the fact
that the "broad *a*" of *father* was completely unknown to
him: *art* and *calm* had in his mouth the vowel of *mat*, *can*.
The "broad *a*," as we learn elsewhere, broke into London
usage about 1780, and later crossed to America. The
diphthong of *foul* he writes as a compound of the vowel of
fall with the vowel of *fool*; either the modern Philadelphia
(and rustic New England) usage had not developed, or it
did not commend itself to him. The group *oi* he does not
mention, nor does he happen to use it in his text. In respect to the third diphthong, that of *eye* or *I*, he gives us
an interesting analysis. "What in our common alphabet
is supposed the third vowel, *i*, as we sound it," he says,
"is as a *diphthong*, consisting of two of our vowels joined;
viz., *u* as sounded in 'unto,' and *i* in its true sound. Any
one will be sensible of this, who sounds those two vowels
. . . quick after each other. . . . The true sound of the *i*
is that we now give to *e* in the words 'deed,' 'keep.'"
Franklin had, then, in such words as *eye*, *fine*, *wind*, the
pronunciation which we now associate with Ireland.
Among the consonants, it is noteworthy that his *r* was always a vibration of "the tip of the tongue" against "the
roof of the mouth"; *far*, *art* he pronounced with the vowel
of *fan* and a vigorously trilled *r*. His *s*, as we have seen,
was of the English rather than the continental European
type. His *t*, *d*, *n*, also, were distinctively English, being
made "by the fore part of the tongue against the roof of
the mouth." His *l*, however, was "formed still more forward, in the mouth, by the tip of the tongue applied first
to the roots of the upper teeth"; probably he had been ob-
serving initial rather than final *l*.

Not without interest are Franklin's renderings of certain individual words. *Are* he always pronounced, it would seem, like *air*, though perhaps shorter. *Get* for him was *git*, *friend* was *frind*; *been* had "short *i*." *Have* and *has*, when unstressed, were *hev* and *hes*. *Bosom* had in its first syllable the vowel of *but*. *Angel* began, it would seem, with the vowel of *end* (which was used also in *change*); but in the writing of *e* and *ee*, our amateur phonetician was careless. In *calm* Franklin sounded the *l*; so he did, apparently, in *could*, *would*, and *should*. *To* was usually identical with *toe*. The word *new*, which occurs repeatedly, is always written "*nu*," indicating the vowel of *noose*; whereas *few* is of course spelled "*fiu*," as *you* is "*iu*" and *use* is "*ius*." Throughout the texts the usage is of an elaborately formal type.

The principles advocated in his unfinished exposition are those which phoneticians now advocate. "Thus the *g*," he says, "has no longer two different sounds, which occasioned confusion, but is, as every letter ought to be, confined to one. The same is to be observed in all the letters, vowels and consonants, that wherever they are met with, or in whatever company, their sound is always the same. It is also intended, that there be *no superfluous* letters used in spelling; that is, no letter that is not sounded; and this alphabet, by six new letters, provides, that there be no distinct sounds in the language *without letters* to express them."

Appended to the interrupted introduction are three samples of the advocated orthography. The first consists of two stanzas from Addison, *The Storm*, at that time a familiar poem. Next comes a short letter from Miss Mary Stevenson, written in "Kensington, 26 September, 1768," criticizing the proposed spelling, but using it (except in her final sentence). Follows, lastly, a longer epistle from Franklin, in reply to Miss Stevenson's strictures. It is interesting to discover that the arguments, on both sides of the question, have undergone no essential change in the course of 158 years. Here is Miss Stevenson's missive, done into the still-current cacography:

"Dear Sir,

"I have transcribed your alphabet, &c., which I think might be of service to those, who wish to acquire an accurate pronunciation, if that could be fixed; but I see many inconveniences, as well as difficulties, that would attend the bringing your letters and orthography into common use. All our etymologies would be lost, consequently we could not ascertain the meaning of many words; the distinction, too, between words of different meaning and similar sound would be useless, unless we living writers publish new editions. In short I believe we must let people spell on in their old way, and (as we find it easiest) do the same ourselves. *With ease and with sincerity I can, in the old way, subscribe myself,*

"*Dear Sir,*
"*Your faithful and affectionate servant,*

M.S."

Now for Franklin's answer, which also is here transcribed:

"Dear Madam:

"The objection you make to rectifying our alphabet, 'that it will be attended with inconveniences and difficulties,' is a natural one; for it always occurs when any reformation is proposed; whether in religion, government, laws, and even down as low as roads and wheel carriages. The true question then, is not whether there will be no difficulties or inconveniences but whether the difficulties may not be surmounted; and whether the conveniences will not, on the whole, be greater than the inconveniences. In this case, the difficulties are only in the beginning of the practice; when they are once overcome, the advantages are lasting. — To either you or me, who spell well in the present mode, I imagine the difficulty of changing that mode for the new, is not so great, but that we might perfectly get over it in a week's writing.—As to those who do not spell well, if the two difficulties are compared, viz., that of teaching them true spelling in the present mode, and that of teaching them the new alphabet and the new spelling according to it, I am confident that the latter would be by far the least. They naturally fall into the new method already, as much as the imperfection of their alphabet will admit of; their present bad spelling is only bad, because contrary to the present bad rules; under the new rules it would be good. — The difficulty of learning to spell well in the old way is so great, that few attain it; thousands and thousands writing on to old age, without ever being able to acquire it. 'T is, besides, a difficulty continually increasing, as the sound gradually varies more and more from the spelling; and to foreigners it makes the learning to pronounce our language, as written in our books, almost impossible.

"Now as to 'the inconveniences' you mention. — The first is, that 'all our etymologies would be lost, consequently we could not ascertain the meaning of many words.' — Etymologies are at present very uncertain, but such as they are, the old books would still preserve them, and etymologists would there find them. Words in the course of time, change their meanings, as well as their spelling and pronunciation; and we do not look to etymology for their present meanings. If I should call a man a knave and a villain, he would hardly be satisfied with my telling him, that one of the words originally signified only a lad or servant; and the other, an under plowman, or the inhabitant of a village. It is from present usage only the meaning of words is to be determined.

"Your second inconvenience is, that 'the distinction between words of different meaning and similar sound would be destroyed.' That distinction is already destroyed in pronouncing them; and we rely on the sense alone of the sentence to ascertain, which of the several words, similar in sound, we intend. If this is sufficient in the rapidity of discourse, it will be much more so in written sentences, which may be read leisurely, and attended to more particularly in case of difficulty, than we can attend to a past sentence, while a speaker is hurrying us along with new ones.

"Your third inconvenience is, that 'all the books already written would be useless.' — This inconvenience would only come on gradually, in a course of ages. You and I, and your own living readers, would hardly forget the use of them. People would long learn to read the old writing, though they practiced the new. — And the inconvenience is not greater, than what has already actually happened in a similar case, in Italy. Formerly its inhabitants all spoke and wrote Latin; as the language changed, the spelling followed it. It is true that, at present, a mere unlearn'd Italian cannot read the Latin books; though they are still read and understood by many. But, if the spelling had never been changed, he would now have found it much more difficult to read and write his own language; for written words would have had no relation to sounds, they would only have stood for things; so that if he would express in writing the idea he has, when he sounds the word *Vescovo*, he must use the letters *Episco-pus*. — In short, whatever the difficulties and inconveniences now are, they will be more easily surmounted now, than hereafter; and some time or other, it must be done; or our writing will become the same with the Chinese, as to the difficulty of learning and using it. And it would already have been such, if we had continued the Saxon spelling and writing, used by our forefathers.

"I am, my dear friend, yours affectionately,

LONDON,   B. FRANKLIN."
CRAVEN-STREET, Sept. 28, 1768.

Eighteen years later, in his own country (at last emancipated), Franklin's views were still the same; for on July 4, 1786, he wrote as follows to Mrs. Jane Mecom: "You need not be concerned, in writing to me, about your bad spelling; for, in my opinion, as our alphabet now stands, the bad spelling, or what is called so, is generally the best, as conforming to the sound of the letters and of the words."

How the good patriot would have sorrowed, had he known that, 150 years after the founding of the Republic, his beloved country, though long since rid of the light yoke of British dominion, had not yet shaken off the crushing yoke of ancient official orthography!

As the Feller Said

I N a Yankee village resides a man who, like the late Latin stylists, is fond of tailing off his periods in a cadence. Every third sentence, with him, ends with the refrain "as the feller said." The dying fall of the phrase so feeds his love that he will undoubtedly play on, thwanging this same string of his lyre until he himself shall die. "No, I don't think it's goin' to clear off. It'll rain before night, as the feller said." "Keep your boat in the water for a week, an' it'll all swell up, as the feller said." "No, I ain't a-goin' to do no more business with him. I'm done with him, as the feller said."

I have compared our villager to a silvery Latin rhetor. Really, in spirit he is medieval. Middle Age writers apparently considered originality a dangerous if not fatal obstacle to a career as best seller. If they had authorities, they cited them (though not always the real ones); if they had none, they invented one, like Wolfram's mysterious Guiot. To be sure, they did sometimes hold out the promise of novelty; but they were very loath, in their subject-matter, to stray far from the shelter of a source. That, no doubt, is why source-hunting has become such a rich sport among philologists. Another reason is that the pursuit offers so many convenient subjects for theses.

"But we have changed all that," as the feller said. Our literary man of today is mortally afraid of letting his "feller" out of the closet. The one thing he most craves is a reputation for invention. Possibly his ideas, or some of them, may come to him directly from Heaven, but no nearer source is admissible. His own seething brain, like the Gold Dust Twins, does the work. Imitation, which used to be held up as a virtue, is now stigmatized as plagiarism — except, of course, imitation of the very latest idol. One may with impunity imitate T. S. Eliot, James Joyce, or Marcel Proust (notice that my word is "may," not "can"); but to exhibit symptoms of the influence of Tennyson, Thackeray, or Hugo puts one beyond the pale.

The Rev. Thomas Jefferson White was dining at the house of his parishioners, Mr. and Mrs. George Washington Remus. "Dis am a mighty fahn goose, Mr. Remus," observed the reverend guest. "Whar you git um?" "Mr. White," replied the host, with dignity, "Ah doan' ask you whar you git your sermons." And right he was: the "feller" must be forgotten.

After all, though, there are two ways of showing originality. An artist may get new things out of old subjects, or he may create new themes. I wonder which demands the greater invention. Homer, Virgil, Dante, Chaucer, Shakspere were contented with the former process. Nothing short of the latter will satisfy the higher standard of the now current generation. "New matter for the new age," is the cry. Of course, every generation is new; but each new one thinks itself newer than any that went before. And in a certain sense it is right. I suppose more plots have been contrived in the last fifty years than the stage ever saw in its whole previous existence. Nevertheless, there seems to have been as much borrowing as ever. "My subject," explained the ambitious young dramatist, "is taken from the French." "Is it?" replied the weary manager, handing back the manuscript. "Well, the French will never miss it."

One novel field of exploitation is the subconscious self.
You go reeling off ream after ream of inconsequent
snatches, mixing it up with some really intelligible inci-
dents and ideas, and present it as the great stream of un-
controlled cerebration that flows constantly just beneath
our consciousness. To be sure, Freud says there is no
such thing as the subconscious, and that is rather dis-
quieting; because, of course, King Freud can say no
wrong. All the same, if there were such a thing as the
subconscious, perhaps it would be something like that;
and it would be mighty interesting to know what people's
subconscious personalities were up to. Of course, nobody
can really tell just what his own subconsciousness is doing
(assuming for the moment that he has one); and it is
quite evident that the enterprising novelist can have no
means whatever of determining the possibly non-existent
subconsciousness of anybody else. The interest, in any
case, would be altogether scientific, rather than esthetic;
and it takes a good deal of enthusiasm to keep the home
fires burning in an investigation of things which, if they
do exist, afford no outward manifestation. One might
conceivably (especially if one had pretty good hope of
scandalous revelations) relish Mr. or Mrs. Smith's confession of what he or she conceived to be his or her subconscious consciousness, but to make a meal of Mr.
Jones's guess about Mr. or Mrs. Smith's subconsciousness requires an uncommonly keen appetite.

Another fresh field is smells. Not quite so fresh as subconsciousness, for it has been tilled since Baudelaire. But
it has not been tilled very much, and may yet reserve
surprises. An interesting characteristic is that it has no
vocabulary of its own; it therefore taxes curiously the in-
geniousness of the cultivator. For that very reason it has

a certain fascination for the author (if he possesses a fertile wit), whatever its effect may be on the reader.

A physician attending a poor negro family was continually annoyed by the misbehavior of its youngest member. Finally he lost patience. "That child is spoiled!" he cried suddenly, pointing at the tiny culprit. "Why, no, doctor," soothingly answered the mother. "All little colored babies smells like dat."

"Jimmie Fadden," said the schoolteacher, "I must send you home at once to get clean. I can't have any boy here as dirty as you are." And she penned a note to the boy's mother: "Please wash Jimmie before you send him back here. He is so untidy that his odor is very offensive." Within a half-hour the youthful Fadden reappeared, still triumphantly unwashed. He bore this missive from his parent: "I want you to keep my boy in school. You was hired to learn Jimmie, not to smell him."

In the grocery store there appeared that afternoon — the afternoon before the show — a tall, pale, long-haired, solemn and rather seedy gentleman, who in a deep voice accosted the grocer: "I should like, me good man, to purchase your whole stock of stale eggs." "Oh, I see!" cried the merry tradesman, "you're goin' to see *Hamlet* in the Town Hall tonight." "No," answered the gloomy stranger, "I am going to act *Hamlet*."

"How can one prevent a fish from smelling?" asked *le bon Roi Dagobert*. "Cut off its nose," replied *le grand Saint Eloi*.

No, this will not do. It is not a bit like Huysmans. Despite their scent of antiquity, these *exempla* do not properly illustrate the style in question. Perhaps one would do better to follow the trail of reminiscent odors.

We are all familiar with the recurrence of half-forgotten

scenes and sounds which suddenly return to the mind (suggested by a subtle connection with something seen or heard in the present) and thus momentarily renew this incident or that of our past lives. Very often, however, these old experiences flash back upon us without the stimulus or sight of hearing; and then we are quite at a loss to account for their unexpected emergence into our consciousness. I suppose there is always something to start them; and that something, I am sure, is frequently a smell. For my own case I have labeled a few of these evasive stimuli — evasive because the sense of smell has been little explored, in comparison with hearing and vision. Touch, also, has been neglected by the literary folk. I should not be surprised to see it soon come into fashion. By the way, I have read somewhere (I do not mean in a novel or a poem, but in some real psychology book) that smell is the first of the senses to grow dull with advancing age. It is not so with me; on the contrary, smell is the one sense of mine that has quite retained its discriminating keenness.

All at once, in some New World *milieu*, I see the streets of old Paris, the Paris of the Latin Quarter half a century and more ago, when I played in the Luxembourg Garden and in the waste lands just at the south of it. That resurrected picture I owe (as I have discovered by repeated experience) to a particular scent, a combination of fruit, vegetables, wine, and humidity.

Suddenly I behold the moon at close range, with a projectile circling around it, or a huge cannon, in Florida, its mouth pointed to the sky. This experience comes to me in a library, or at home, when I open certain special books. For they preserve the odor made dear to me by the beautifully illustrated volumes of Jules Verne's *De la*

terre à la lune and *Autour de la lune*, which were presented
to me on my twelfth birthday. My poor little playmate,
Marie, was never allowed to read them, her very competent governess having inferred from an examination of
the cuts that the text was presumably not at all points in
accord with accepted fact.

Even now the smell of dry, dusty horse dung (rare
enough nowadays, though once all-pervasive in our
streets) gives me a sense of guilt. Listen to my confession.
I must have been about five. A tiny companion and I
had fallen out. He was a very dear and very gentle child.
I cannot understand how we quarreled so violently; indeed, I greatly fear the violence was all on my side. Anyhow, the struggle ended with a push so successful that it
sent my antagonist rolling into the middle of the pavement, whence he arose thickly coated with the substance
just mentioned. Nay, more: to my remorseful eyes, at
least, the big, slow tears seemed to plough their way
through a similar coating on his cheeks. How I brushed
and brushed, with hand, with cap, even with handker-
chief (mine, not his), while he stood like Niobe! No re-
proach came from his lips; but what rebuke could have
cut my heart like his silent grief? Brush as I would, the
telltale aroma remained. It clung to him as the breath of
the springtime clings to the crushed rose. Brush, brush,
brush! Madly and more madly, as anguish deepened to
despair. I could not even detect a diminution of the
horsy smell. At that inopportune moment I espied my
father advancing along the sidewalk. Down to my boots
went my terror-stricken heart. He, however, had seen
nothing. He spoke to us with his wonted kindness, taking
each of us by the hand. My father was exceedingly fond
of children; but he had an unreasonable habit of assuming

I was in the wrong, whenever I had a row with anybody.
On this occasion he invited us to walk along with him.
We must have been an unresponsive pair. Willy had not
really recovered his voice; from time to time his chest
would give a convulsive heave, and a few dilatory tears
would slowly exude like the last drops of blood from the
Dying Gladiator. As for me, I was so full of fright and
so choked with wickedness that I could scarcely hear,
let alone converse. My father, all unsuspecting, chatted
merrily. Above everything else in my consciousness was
that damning smell of horse manure. Stronger and
stronger it grew; it stifled me; I thought it must suffocate
the world. Could it be that my father did not detect it?
Was he pretending, in order to make my punishment
more terrible? Would his affectionate *badinage* suddenly
turn to merciless irony? From moment to moment I expected to see his face change; I expected him to halt
abruptly, and sniff. Next would come the dread inquiry;
whereupon Willy, with reluctance no doubt, but with
painful preciseness (for he was a truthful boy) would out
with the whole horrible tale. Then the *Dies Iræ;* then
would my father smite me — euphemistically speaking —
hip and thigh. The suspense was wellnigh unbearable.
Like the murderer in Poe's *Telltale Heart,* I wanted to
shriek out: "Dissemble no longer!" Spanking seemed
sweet, compared to this. "La tema si volge in disio." Still
that smell! Still my father smelt it not. He never noticed
it, even to the end. By good fortune, the end came soon;
for after three blocks my father had to leave us and take a
car. My crime remained undiscovered. I have never confessed it until this moment, when, as I sit here, the fatal
scent (or the memory of it) is in some mysterious manner
wafted to my nostrils. Thus repeats itself the story of
Eugene Aram, the story of *The Bells.*

There is no doubt of it. All unknown to us, odors influence our whole *Weltanschauung*. Pictures, too, exert their spell. A friend of mine, when he was a small child, was fond of poring over the family Bible and always studied with particular interest a certain illustration containing a figure — a strange shape — which he unquestioningly took to be God the Father. And all through life his conception of the Divinity was vaguely colored by this idea. Only at a very mature age, happening to look over the old pictures, did he discover that the strange figure in question was evidently intended for a camel.

Most people who concern themselves with Dante conceive of his character in accordance with some picture of him which they have seen in their early years. Do they think of him as a "pale young curate" of the Anglican Church? They presumably have in the back of their heads the Giotto fresco in the Bargello. If their impressionable age was stamped by the so-called "death mask," their Dante is a powerful and gloomy sufferer who never had a childhood or a youth, and never cracked a smile. Those (and they are many) for whom he was a pitiless hater, a rabid anti-clerical who sent all the Popes to Hell, are under the spell of Raphael's fiendish invention. As for myself, I had the good fortune to see often on our parlor table, in a copy of Cary's translation with Flaxman's drawings, a frontispiece which strikingly reminded me of Miss Mary Talbot. Now Miss Talbot was a very dear lady, a great friend of my mother's, a sufferer from cruel rheumatism, and perhaps for that reason the more sympathetic with my ills. During my convalescence from measles, from scarlet fever, from diphtheria she would sit cheeringly by my bedside and accompany me in play with my toys. So fond was I of her that Cary's

Dante, with its portrait of Miss Talbot, became one of my favorite books while I was still at the initial stage of the art of reading. And even now I cannot quite dissociate Alighieri from the wise gentleness of that sweet comforter who, *non ignara mali*, had learned to succor the unhappy — as the feller said.

Ourselves and Others

Suave, mari magno turbantibus æquora ventis,
E terra magnum alterius spectare laborem.

TRUE! nobody can deny it. But why? Why do we love to sit comfortably on the shore and contemplate other people's nautical distresses? Does the sight of their peril really enhance the enjoyment of our own security? Or is it a case of Aristotelian catharsis? Or is that, perhaps, what catharsis means? Anyhow, we purge our emotions vicariously, and we like it. For my own part, I suspect it is pure cussedness; it is the old Adam in us, the same spirit of contrariness that moved the head of our house to break the only rule he had.

That very same tendency makes us ready to gulp down any gossip detrimental to our neighbor, no matter how unlikely it may be, or how notoriously mendacious the reporter. We accept a bit of slander, unquestioningly, from a person to whom we should never entrust a nickel without long and painful consideration. At most, when we repeat the libel, we introduce it by some such formula as "People on the inside are saying . . ." or "Someone in a position to know has told me . . ." All the while, what we really know, in spite of our frantic efforts at deglutition, is that the whole yarn is unswallowable nonsense. But why do we so furiously want to believe it? Do we derive a tottering sense of superiority from supposititious evidence of the turpitude of our friends and associates? More probably it is sheer malice, which ordinarily con-

tents itself with words and only in abnormal cases trans-
lates itself into acts. We all have more or less of the Iago
in us.

Years ago, I was acquainted with a lady lunatic. She
was a pretty little lady, somewhere in her fifties, well bred
and soft-spoken, a pathetic figure, though in manner
habitually cheerful. Sometimes wearisomely persistent
in her autobiographical confidences, she was otherwise
harmless, and roamed at large, performing unofficially the
function of a liaison officer in the community where I was
staying. Did I say "harmless"? The poor creature, I am
sure, meant no harm. But, like other crazy people, she
had grievances; she had been, and was, darkly and direly
persecuted. And the persecutors, though not always identical, had this in common, that they were always people
in the same set. Stories that would have done credit
to that ingenious cavalier, the Baron von Münchhausen,
were thus carried from house to house, and things flesh-
creepily wicked or (less often) angelically good were related of the Blacks to the Browns, of the Browns to the
Whites, of the Whites to the Grays, of the Grays to the
Greens. How were these tales received? Of course one
had to listen indulgently to the poor mad chatterbox; and
one rejected out of hand, as the fruit of a diseased brain,
all the disinterested and heroic deeds attributed to the
Blacks, the Browns, the Whites, the Grays, or the
Greens. As to the infamous, dastardly, inhuman, criminal doings of these same Blacks, Browns, Whites, Grays,
and Greens, — their plots, their robberies, their murders,
— one naturally found it impossible to accept them in all
their luridness; yet one suspected (and the suspicion continually grew) that somewhere at the bottom there must
be a germ of truth. On reflection, the Blacks could re-

member having detected a certain shady tinge in the Browns, the Browns had more than once been startled into a perception that the Whites were not so spotless as they seemed, the Whites had occasionally found the Grays a bit hard to classify, the Grays had long harbored a doubt of the verdant innocence of the Greens. No, the unfortunate little lady could not have invented everything out of whole cloth; and her feverish outpourings, fantastic though they might be, explained a good deal of the feeling — a queer, uncomfortable feeling — one had always experienced in the proximity of the Blacks, the Browns, the Whites, the Grays, and the Greens. It is always safer to be on one's guard. By adding one thing to another, one arrived cumulatively at a juster estimate of people. Thus households are split, thus family feuds are started, thus wars are made.

What is more natural than suspicion? It is based on a sense of mental or moral superiority, and its exercise strengthens that satisfactory sentiment. A policeman was conducting to the station a wrongdoer whom he had arrested — an "alleged" wrongdoer, as the newspapers say (suspicious even of crime). During the transit, the culprit's hat blew off, and he asked his captor for permission to chase it. "No, ye don't!" cried exultingly the Guardian of the Law, closing one of his shrewd eyes. "No, ye're not goin' to play that game on me. I know your tricks. Now, you stand right here, an' I'll go after your hat."

Give a nation a bad name, and then make war on it. What is more impressive than a long row of ciphers? And yet, despite their collective fury, each one of them is as a tale told by an idiot. We begin by attributing to a people a trait that one of the aforesaid gentry may have affixed to it, and then we go through life rolling up corroborative evidence. Anything that is ever done, or is said to be done, by anybody private or any body politic is susceptible of interpretation in accordance with the opinion we have preconceived of that individual or communal entity, whatever the gratuitous opinion may be. Let Cæsar weep at the cry of the poor: to his partisan he appears as a tender philanthropist; to his opponent, a theatrical politician. Let a President, in his vacation, use earthworms for bait, and he will find himself both an exemplar of sane and unspoiled native simplicity and a *poseur* fishing for rural votes rather than for trout.

The Scotch are thrifty. We have it on the word of *Punch*, who without their thrift would find existence sorely straitened. But *Punch's* voice is only one of many. Indeed, the Caledonian repute is so widespread that it had even reached the ears of that Pittsburgh multimillionaire who went over, three summers ago, to play golf on golf's native heath. Safely reinstated in Pittsburgh, after a sufficient round of sport abroad, — he never wearied — the verb is here used intransitively — he never wearied, I say, of relating his exploits *in extenso*. And especially did he love to dilate on the proverbial Scottish parsimony.

"You would never believe," he declared impressively, "that any people could be so miserly. They cling on to a penny as if it was a million dollars. I'll just give you an illustration. At St. Andrew's, one morning, I had got to the first tee and was all ready to play, when my pipe went out. Of course I could n't be seen playing without my pipe; all the papers had my picture with it. But when I tried to light up, I found I had n't any matches. There happened to be nobody around I could borrow one of;

but not far off, fortunately, there was a little tobacco shop. I hurried in and asked for a light. But what did the proprietor do but hand me a box of matches and say 'tuppence.' 'Why, I don't want a whole box of matches,' says I; 'I just want one match, to light my pipe.' 'Tuppence,' says he. 'See here,' says I, beginning to get hot under the collar. 'You don't seem to understand. I ain't going to buy no box of matches. I've got a box in my other clothes. I just want a light for my pipe. In any tobacco-shop in my country they give you a light for nothing.' 'Tuppence,' says he again, still holding out the box. And, will you believe it? I had to walk a mile and a half back to my hotel to get a light!"

Verily, the Scot is unco canny (I am not quite sure what "unco" means, but I know it is an indispensable word if you are out for Scottish color). However, canny though he be, the Scot probably has his good side. Everybody has a good side, if you go round and round him. As has been said before, "God made Scotland." I have never heard who made Pittsburgh. Be open to favorable impressions, and give the other fellow the benefit of the doubt. He probably needs it. Remember that even the burglar "loves to lie a-basking in the sun." "Was your lawyer a good one?" a friend asked the defendant, after the trial. "Good? I should say he was. Why! he not only got me acquitted, but he convinced me I was innocent." That is the spirit: think the best of people, and then stick to it.

Many years ago, I heard from the President of Mt. Holyoke the following incident in the career of a Wellesley girl — a freshman, no doubt. It was an English composition course, and the student had handed in a theme on "Why I Like College," wherein, with youthful optimism, she had declared: "I think the Wellesley Faculty are just lovely." Opposite this, the unfeeling corrector had written "feeble!!!" And the authoress had been directed to rewrite the whole. Observe the effectiveness of sweet pertinacity! In the amended version, the crucial passage read thus: "The Wellesley Faculty may be feeble, but they are lovely just the same."

Windows

W E need never be alone. The lonely man is he who gazes too absorbedly within, and finds not there the companionship he craves; the world-weary mortal is weary not of the world, but of himself, in whom his world exists. To find ourselves objects of live interest — ready, on encouragement, to turn into sympathy — we have but to look about us. If we dwell in the midst of humanity, we may be sure that every day brings us into contact with fellow-creatures eager to know more of us and to let us know more of them; for sociability, in our kind, is always quivering with desire to burst the bonds of shyness, curiosity is constantly at grips with fear. If we go out into the wilderness, our experience is the same: we presently become aware of bright little eyes peering inquisitively from the dark; and, if we remain long motionless, soft little feet, disobeying the summons to flight, will gradually creep closer and closer, throbbing little hearts will vanquish their habitual terror — so powerful is the lure of the unknown. The rabbit who risks his life to make our acquaintance is moved by the same spirit which impels the explorer to the frozen pole.

Yes, the lower animals (as we superbly denominate them) have their portion of scientific curiosity — that is, the impulse to acquire knowledge merely for the sake of knowing. Yes, they have it; but their facilities are poor for the cultivation of it. When not inhibited by fear, their tendency to original research is oftenest checked by utilitarian considerations. It flashes out now and then, but the results of its observation can (as far as we know) be neither recorded nor transmitted. Man alone (as far as we know) has speech; and only a part of mankind has writing. The means of accumulation, communication, and perpetuation are ours but not theirs; and we, not they, can humor to the top of its bent the instinctive thirst for knowledge. Yet that instinct is in them; it reaches down deeper than humanity.

Without it, perhaps, humanity had never been. Who can tell which had the greater share in the evolution of our race — necessity or curiosity? Hard enough it is to say what is the motive of a single specific act. At any rate, these twain, necessity and curiosity, the impulse to stay alive and the impulse to learn, are the propelling forces in our development. To them we owe what we have and what we are.

The appetite for knowledge grows by what it feeds on. The more we know, the more we inquire, and the more painful ignorance becomes. Even going back no further than some of us can remember, how rapid has been the decrease of things which everybody was content to leave in blackness! Swift as the passing of the moon's shadow from the face of the sun has been the spread of light over dark places. To some, this impatient quest for enlightenment has seemed the dominant trait of our kind. Through it, they declare, man became man and is becoming — who knows what?

"All men," says Aristotle at the beginning of his *Metaphysics*, "naturally desire to know." "The reason whereof may be," explains Dante, who takes this passage to introduce his *Banquet*, "that everything in the universe, stamped by nature with a character of its own, is irresistibly impelled to work out its peculiar perfection; and inasmuch as the ultimate perfection of man is knowledge, that is what we men constantly crave to acquire." So intensely do we crave it that we — many of us, at least — are willing to sacrifice comfort and pleasure and safety, even life, to find the answers to our puzzles. What land should we now inhabit, were that not so? Not America, surely. For while, no doubt, various causes drove Columbus — or whoever discovered our continent — across the sea, it is impossible not to believe that the supreme motive was eagerness to penetrate uncharted space. That same eagerness, never assuaged, binds the astronomer, night after night, year after year, to exploration of the useless stars. The ravening, universal hunger for information, even information of no importance, just because it is or purports to be information, keeps our newspapers alive.

What is to come of it? Can it be that man, possessed by this insatiable demon, curiosity — possessed also of means of imparting and storing all that he wins — can it be that some day he shall come to know everything? And, if so, what field can there then be for his favorite activity? Will he cease to be man when he shall no longer be on the hunt, having already got all that there is? To know everything! Everything is a good deal. But even aside from the immensity of the knowable, the infinite magnitude of the objective, we need have no fear of repleteness; we find in ourselves wherewith to allay our dread of the denaturing of man by omniscience. There are obstacles. Not external barriers alone, such as the Atlantic offered to Columbus, or meaningless millions of light-years to the astronomer; these may conceivably all be surmounted. No: inner impediments, hindrances that we create for ourselves. In our race for science, we carry with us our own supply of hurdles, which trip us sooner or later. These obstacles it is my purpose to discuss. Let us begin by changing our metaphor.

Every one of us has a house, full of many rooms, and every room has windows. In some of these windows the blinds are up, and the sunshine streams through; others have their shutters closed, and darkness reigns within. Most of you remember the "parlor" or the "best room" in the old-fashioned rural New England home: never opened save for weddings and funerals, dank, musty, suffocating, shrouded in a perpetual night that seems impervious to the sun's ray. Such are the closed rooms in our mental house. For we all have some of these clammy interiors; seldom or never have I seen a habitation all of whose windows invited the day.

Why must this be? Why, for instance, do I keep the blinds down in the four back rooms on my second story and one front room on my ground floor? The answer is simple: because other people do it. To leave all one's windows open would be eccentric; it simply is not done. Furthermore, fashion selects the rooms that must be darkened; I have little to say about it. Fashion! that fickle, flitting goddess, whose moods are so brief, so variable, but so imperious while they last! The windows in question are victims of collectivism. For it is collective opinion, not mine, that rules in those apartments and forbids their illumination.

Recently, in Cambridge, we have seen the disinterment of an old phrase which was alive in my undergraduate days — "Harvard indifference." The expression is now happily dead, and the present attempt at revivification only shows how dead it is. A year or two ago, a couple of our student debating teams discussed the problem whether "Harvard indifference" is a good or a bad thing. But they cherished diametrically different ideas about the meaning of the term. One set of debaters defined it in one way, and accordingly defended it; the other, giving it a totally opposed significance, held it up to reprobation. But I can remember when it really stood for something — something sinister and abnormal: namely, an attitude of *blasé*, world-weary aloofness from all the feelings and doings of mankind. I say an attitude, for that is what it was. Such aloofness never can really exist in the young — nay, nor in the old, either, if the truth be told. It was a pose, a mask prescribed by fashion. But a pose long maintained inevitably comes to influence not only the conduct but also the character of the *poseur;* it strikes in. The haughtily elevated eyebrow begets a prematurely and permanently wrinkled forehead and a crinkled disposition. The affectedly unseeing eye turns really half blind. The young men who assumed such affectation, who subjected themselves to the inconvenience and the disastrous consequences of such a pose, were in fact sacrificing themselves to fashion; they were offering their own selves, or portions of their own selves, as victims to Collective Opinion, an Authority which bade them keep their windows shut.

With most of us the tyrant is less exacting: he allows us to have some of our shutters open; but he is a tyrant, none the less. There was a time, not so long ago, when we thought of Free Will as the greatest of man's possessions, the divinest of God's gifts to humanity. How jealously we guarded it, how enraptured we were to snatch any scrap of it from Predestination! In later, less theological days, the rôle of Predestination is played by Heredity and Environment, which, under scientific direction, hedge in our liberty on every hand and already proclaim that they have annihilated our freedom of choice. Yet we will not, we cannot believe it! Impotent machines we are not. Some fragment of Free Will must be left us, despite all the encroachments of Predestination, Heredity, and Environment. That little bit of liberty we shall defend with our lives: it is our most precious treasure, our Palladium! But, no! at any moment we are ready to offer it up as a sacrifice to Conformity.

Especially ready are we in this land of standardization, the land of the flivver, the land where everybody's main ambition is to be exactly like everybody else. Such uniformity can be attained by discarding all that is individual in each one of us and keeping only the residuum that is common to the race. Standardization and Organization are our twin gods, Organization being our saviour in time of need, our plague at the vastly more numerous times when it is not needed. During the greater part of our lives we organize just for the sake of organizing. If two Americans should be cast up on a desert island, they would straightway proceed to organize a society with a president and a secretary-treasurer; then they would try to think of something for their society to do. Their situation unfortunately would debar them from the usual resource of associations similarly perplexed: they could not well send out a questionnaire. A questionnaire is a device for causing the greatest possible amount of trouble to the largest possible number of people. It is supposed to organize collective opinion.

Now, collective opinion is very often right; but, then, on the other hand, it is very often wrong. "Collective opinion, right or wrong" is a dangerous motto. It leads

us to close not only the windows which our own particular
feebleness would prefer to keep shut, but all those, as
well, whose openness might let in too much light on the
collective weaknesses of humanity.

Let us return for a moment to Aristotle. According to
his philosophy, the powers of the individual mind are restricted to concrete things — sensations, perceptions, and
the like; when we launch out into abstract thought, we
have to unite with a great, external, active intelligence,
the νοῦς ποιητικός — the mind that does things, or, in
Emersonian terminology, the Oversoul. This Oversoul,
or Collective Intelligence, is the thinker; it is the Active
One. Now, the startling fact is this: the ancient Greeks
used to unite with their Collective Intelligence in order to
think, whereas we make connection with our Collective
Opinion in order not to think. We let it do our thinking
for us without our coöperation.

Why do we so hate to think? It is, to be sure, a painful process, for one who is not accustomed to it. It forces
him spiritually into the attitude that is physically por-
trayed in Rodin's statue of "Le Penseur." Even for one
who has the habit, reflection is difficult on a subject on
which one has not reflected before, especially a subject on
which one has hitherto accepted a judgment ready-made.
But indolence, natural shrinking from the labor and the
childbirth pains of an idea — this is not our only reason
for abstinence. Perhaps it is not our principal reason.
For, beside it, there is fear. We are afraid to think, lest
we think something different, something original and
therefore eccentric, something that may make us stand
out from the rest. To be distinguished is to be ridiculous.
Better submit than attract the pointing finger. Even in
such a trivial and intimate matter as the proper date for

assuming a straw hat or putting it aside, we dare not trust our own judgment. All straw hats must be put on at the same moment, and at the same moment all must be taken off. Until the day therefor shall have been fixed by a constitutional amendment (as it surely will be ere long), Collective Opinion will legislate, and will see that its legislation is enforced; for Collective Opinion allows no infraction of its law. Samuel Butler was right when, in *Erewhon*, he represented Mrs. Grundy as the only power, human or superhuman, that is really feared and obeyed. She even tells us how we shall name our daughters; for in these United States, as you may have observed, all the girl-children born in a given twelvemonth have to be named alike, the appellation changing from year to year — one season Eleanor, another Gladys, another Alison: a habit that is bound to become embarrassing to ladies who see themselves dated by their name-year, and that name-year receding further and further into the past.

After all, though, we have not attained the maximum of organization and uniformity. Look at the ant! There is a creature which realizes our ideal. There is the perfection of conformity. We have all read of that ant which has been found embedded in amber, where it has remained (so the scientists assure us) thirty millions of years; and yet it looks precisely like an ant of today. I am a bit skeptical about these geological figures: possibly the insect may have dwelt in amber only twenty-nine million years; but the lesson is the same. Here is a creature which twenty-nine million years ago achieved a perfect organization, and consequently has not changed since; for the last twenty-nine million years it has kept on doing exactly the same things in exactly the same way. A triumph of standardization! Can mankind hope to match that? Can we venture to look forward to twenty-nine million years of unbroken conformity? At any rate, we can do our best; and we seem to be doing it.

Indolence and cowardice: these are the agents Mrs. Grundy employs to enforce her decrees. "But," asks the spirit of inquiry (if the inquiring spirit still survives), "why have the laws been enacted? Why should Collective Opinion forbid the opening of windows, and why should it tolerate certain windows rather than others?" This is a hard question to answer, the more so as we apparently must answer it in the dark. I suppose the word that explains most of the phenomena is Inertia. We are used to living a great part of our lives in the shadow, and are shy of the light. We are, to be sure, not yet like those cave-fishes which, from dwelling constantly in blackness, have lost the sense of sight. No, we can see; but we think an increase of brightness may hurt our eyes and disturb our habits. And habits do not like to be disturbed. In human conduct, as in physics, a power is required to overcome inertia. Windows do not open themselves. To hoist the blind, we need a curiosity more powerful than the force of custom; and it must be properly applied — it must be turned upon the shut windows, instead of being all deflected to the open ones. We must be convinced there is something to see that we have never seen — something worth seeing, some light without which our house will never be wholly habitable. The inertia which we get from membership in our race must be conquered. Such a victory demands that we keep constant watch of other people's windows and that we take frequent inventory of our own. What are others acquiring that we possess not? What unused possibilities have we in ourselves?

It is not enough, however, to become aware that something is shut; we must have the will to open it, and that will must be more than a match for the will not to open, which we call prejudice. "All men naturally desire to know," says Aristotle. True; but it is true also that all men naturally desire not to know. There are rooms which we wish full of sunlight; there are others to whose illumination we are indifferent; there are others still which we mightily desire to keep dark. These last are the ones that contain our self-indulgences, our sophistries, our pet antipathies and pet superstitions, our cherished beliefs and preferences. Most of these we share with the community in which we live, and they are protected by their prevalence. Others we conceive to be more or less peculiar to ourselves; in these we take pride, the pride of authorship, and we glory in their cultivation. To whichever class it belong, prejudice is a stubborn enemy of freedom, a lover of shade; and prejudice is often abetted by self-interest.

Let us imagine a concrete instance. Here is a man of science, let us say, who has achieved distinction by defending a particular theory. All his career has been devoted to the accumulation of facts to fortify his view, to barricade every avenue of approach. Along comes another scientific man who breaks through the barricades, having discovered or concocted evidence which disproves the aforesaid theory. What will be the reaction of scientist number one? Will he rush into his partially lighted room and throw the blind still further open? Will he join his colleague in the endeavor to let in all the light that can enter? Or will he draw the curtains tighter and devote the rest of his life to recrimination and criticism, to the task of picking flaws in the evidence adduced by his successful rival?

Or, to change the problem a little, let us eliminate the second scholar. Let us suppose that Professor A, after working year in, year out, to gather arguments in support of his opinion, suddenly discovers that his data, if logically arrayed, prove just the opposite. What is now to be his course? Shall it be more light, or less? Shall he confess his error and frankly set forth his reasons for a change of view? Or shall he try to persuade himself — and others — that the evidence may be interpreted as before, and proceed by cunning manipulation to coax his facts to an irrational conclusion?

For the scientific investigator substitute a philosopher, a man of letters, an artist, a musician. A similar situation may arise, with an essentially identical problem. Prejudice and self-interest may join hands, as before. Does the philosopher who adheres to a school really want to get at the inwardness of a different type of speculation? Can the literary man or the artist or the musician see all the merits of a style fundamentally divergent from his own?

Assume that the element of self-interest is reduced to a minimum. Picture a fervently religious man, a layman, with no material stake in his church, but a genuine zeal for it. Other sects he knows, he has to deal with their members, he tries to be fair in his judgment of them, perhaps he goes as far as a critical examination of their creeds. But hardly can he study their dogmas in the same light as his own. Inevitably, or almost inevitably, he lacks the will to see in the rival church the utmost good of which it is capable. Comparing it, consciously or unconsciously, with the religion of his choice, his attention lingers on all the outward blemishes of the first and all the inner beauties of the second; he sees the face of the one, the heart of the other.

Let us pass to the field of politics and consider, not a politician, but an ordinary voter, something of a party man, as most voters are. Behold a candidate antagonistic to his party. This candidate, perhaps, is an innovator, possibly a philanthropist, even a fanatic, who is exposing himself to hardship and contumely in an endeavor to benefit his fellow-creatures. Of his good intentions our voter will hear nothing; of his real ideas and projects our citizen will know nothing. He means to vote against the man, anyhow; and he can do so with greater alacrity if he has no understanding of him. What he wants is a newspaper caricature of a monster of iniquity and folly. A comic cartoon suits him best; and he pulls down the curtain on anything that might blur the impression he has derived therefrom. A pity it is — a thousand times a pity — that we cannot be satisfied to vote against a man merely because we disagree with his method of attaining the same end we ourselves have in view, which is, in general, the welfare of the community. More than once I have been sorely tempted to cast my vote for a candidate or a policy that I thoroughly disapproved, because I was so indignant at the reckless effort to malign the man and obscure the issue. But such indignation may itself be a blind.

Violent emotion, though it may occasionally open our minds to unexpected light, usually is a closer of windows, for it dominates the judgment and the will to believe. In time of war, human nature being what it is, truth has to go by the board, inasmuch as warfare generates intense love and intense hate. Its good effect is a spirit of self-sacrifice and exaltation of faith; the price we have to pay is partial blindness. Not until the fighting is over do the shutters begin to open in narrow chinks, and the day that penetrates is sometimes painful to the long-shadowed eye.

Similar results arise from any fierce conflict, be it a strife of philosophies, of scientific or economic theories, of religious creeds, of racial rivalries, of political parties. The real partisan is unlike the traditional man from Missouri, in that he does not "want to be shown." More philosophic, indeed, is the genuine skeptic, if there be such a person — for most skepticism is an affectation. The favorite phrase of Montaigne, "que sais-je?" is a confession of intellectual modesty, and, if it be sincere, is an indication that the sunshine is nowhere excluded.

Let us turn to matters in which there is no plain question of right and wrong — or, as it is now the fashion to say, "ethical" and "unethical." — matters of dress, let us say, or of pronunciation, or of spelling. By the way, why is it that present-day phraseology gives the name "unethical" to that which used to be plain "wicked"? Is it because "wicked" implies some religious belief, while the modern term testifies to the substitution of "ethical culture"? Or is it simply, as the elder Mr. Weller said of "circumscribed" as compared with "circumwented," that "unethical" is "a more tenderer word"?

Be that as it may, there are in our homes certain obscurations to which one is not immediately disposed to take exception on moral grounds. There are certain subjects which, apparently, it has not been good form to discuss, although the topics are harmless enough in themselves and consideration of them might conceivably lead to improvement.

One of these is pronunciation. Here we must make a distinction. People are quite willing to cite the peculiarities of other people's utterance simply as matters of curiosity or even of scientific interest, just as they have no objection to a study of the anatomy and habits of an ape. But they draw the line at a similar exhibition of their own oddities, or at a comparison of the intrinsic merits of their usage with that of other localities. Such a parallel implies the possibility that other practices may be as good as theirs, or, indeed, distinctly better. Vanity is touched; and vanity is an instantaneous and automatic curtain-dropper. As well debate the question whether man is in all respects superior to the ape and has nothing to regret in the process of evolution — assuming, of course, that he ever had the indiscretion to evolve.

Yet the question of language is in urgent need of asking, for I assure you that some of us are rapidly returning to the linguistic status of our simian progenitor. For some years, at the annual meetings of a great national association, I have heard educated men from various parts of our country, professors of rhetoric, philologists, phoneticians, holding forth in a curious complex of snorts, grunts, and nasal pipes which at first I failed to recognize as human speech, and which even now I am unwilling to call English. Perhaps, after all, Mencken is right when he declares that we no longer speak English, but have developed a language of our own, which he would call "American." If that be true, let us by all means go the whole distance: let us return all the way to the ancestral ape and take a fresh evolutionary start. One of the greatest of American teachers, when he retired from service, announced that he meant to devote the rest of his life to correcting, in himself, the three pernicious consequences of his profession: long-windedness, conceit, and nasality.

Language has many faces. Pronunciation is not the

only one; there is also spelling. The moment that word is uttered, hearers begin to bristle, for the bare mention of it points to a room which all well-ordered households keep darkened, as if a dead body were lying there. The admission of the tiniest ray of light seems an act of profanation. One may, with circumspection, discuss the foundations of religious belief. With considerably more circumspection, one may perhaps examine the principles of government and the structure of society — although, in point of fact, I cannot remember anyone doing so, of late years, without being called a bolshevik. But no amount of caution will redeem an inquiry into the merits of orthography, unless it be the orthography of some foreign tongue or of some very remote period. Of course we all have to occupy ourselves with spelling; it fills an excessively large place in our lives. But we faithfully restrict ourselves to a more or less successful attempt to learn by heart the notations that happen to be conventional in our own country and our own generation, shielding our eyes with blinders from any glimpse into the practices of generations before. Historical perspective is tabu; so is philosophical doubt concerning the divine inspiration of contemporary usage; so is any comparison of the theoretical or practical advantages of different types of alphabetical symbolism. Here is a belief in which everybody is a fundamentalist. Of all other trees in the garden of knowledge we may eat — in due moderation; but this fruit is forbidden. This is the one dark closet which Bluebeard allows no one to open.

We are on the threshold of a special suite of shadowy apartments, the store-rooms of illusion. Now, illusions may be very horrible pests, big with hatefulness, disaster, and death. On the other hand, they may be, and in our

day generally are, innocuous imaginings, often beneficent.
Surely at our present stage we could never endure life
without them; therefore we must for a while indulge ourselves in a few curtained windows in our garret, allowing
the rats to scamper there undisturbed. Illusion, like a
friendly veil, softens the hard lines and sharp corners of
existence. The belief, or half-belief, in things that are
not reconciles us to the acceptance of the things that are.
Illusion is the restful dark boudoir into which we retreat
from the uncompromising white glare of reality. No, we
are not yet ready to give it up. Perhaps, when we shall
see a great deal more of the truth, it will look to us so
beautiful that we shall desire naught else; but that day is
not ours.

Illusions, like prejudices, are unevenly distributed.
Some are wellnigh, if not quite, universal. Some belong
to this or that nation or social group; some to isolated individuals. The astounding fact about them is the tenac-
ity with which we cling to them, in the face of reason and
evidence. Indeed, the presence of destructive evidence
and the absence of logic seem to make the heart grow
fonder. Who is it that believes in the moon as an arbiter
of weather? Who assures you, despite the experience of
millions of moons, that the new moon will bring a me-
teorological change? The farmer! The farmer, who, more
than anyone else, should be concerned with the accuracy
of his prognostications. Who declares to you that rain
will come with the turn of the tide, and is serenely un-
affected by its failure to do so? The fisherman, who, of all
persons, ought to know. Who tells you astounding tales
of porcupines shooting their quills? The hunter, who is
not a plain liar, but really believes what he is saying.
Suppose you own a dog, and your dog bites me. And sup-

pose I go to you and say: "You ought to dispose of that dog; he is a menace to the community. Nobody has a right, merely for his own gratification, to keep a beast that spoils the peace of mind and endangers the lives of his neighbors." My words would make no impression; you would find answers to all my charges, and sufficient justification for preserving your pet. But were I to say: "You must kill the animal, because if he at any time in the future should go mad, I should have hydrophobia," you would have nothing to say. The dog would be doomed. What reason and fact could never achieve, illusion accomplishes in an instant.

Once, when I was a very small boy, I found in a children's book a picture that fascinated me. A dark, dire, dreadful picture, which appealed to all that was romantic in my disposition. A black sky, streaked with white, jagged lines. A black, tumultuous, threatening ocean. Between the two, a ship, evidently in the last stages of distress, scudding under bare poles. Underneath was a mysterious, deliciously unintelligible legend: "The Equinoctial." After long study of the picture and long puzzling over the inscription, I ran to my nurse and asked the meaning of that strange word. The Equinoctial, she told me, was an awful thing which nobody, not even the wisest men, could explain. A storm, worse than all the other storms of the year put together, which always fell on the same day, the twenty-first of September. Why it should inevitably come on that day was beyond comprehension, but come it inevitably did. That was enough for me. I can still remember the delightful shudder which the word Equinoctial always gave me after that. Indeed, I can still shudder it, if the word be spoken in the good old shuddery way. But my faith is fled. I have no wish to undermine the belief of others. I know men who have lost their confidence in immortality, yet still take comfort in their unshaken credence in the Equinoctial Storm. That faith I have lost. Rather should I confess that I have thrown it away, destroyed it by my own rash act. Under Satanic prompting I took note of September 21 and the adjacent days over a series of years; and the Equinoctial Storm returned to fairyland whence it had come. Most men are wiser than I: by keeping their eyes closed at the critical season, they retain their belief and thus their happiness. They can still shudder with a clear conscience.

Do not infer that I apply to all things this spirit of ruthless inquiry. Scientific pedagogy has taught us that habits acquired in one line of conduct are not automatically transferred to others. So-and-So will scoff at ladders but will turn pale at the prospect of sitting down with twelve companions. His neighbor, always careful not to pass beneath a ladder, will treat the fateful number as disdainfully as does that well-known Mr. Lewis who is called by his friends Lewis XIV, because he is invited only to dinner parties at which there would otherwise be thirteen.

One article in the creed of superstitions is, I believe, accepted, explicitly or tacitly, by all, including myself: namely, that ill luck follows any exultation over long-continued good fortune. There are two manifest reasons for the prevalence of this conviction: one is the primitive assumption that the universe is ruled by a malignant power, jealous of human happiness — an assumption which we have never completely outgrown; the other is that the superstition in question is so often justified by experience. Earthly life being thickly sprinkled with ills, a long immunity — from colds, let us say — almost invariably means that a new one is swiftly approaching. It is useless to comfort ourselves with the statement that in matters of luck the past has no influence on the future — that, for instance, throwing double sixes eight times running in no wise affects our chance of a double six at the next throw; we receive this scientific dictum with due respect, but we simply do not believe it. Furthermore, a continued career of prosperity begets recklessness, and recklessness invites disaster. With the downfall comes a sense of pride humiliated; for nothing we actually accomplish makes us quite so vain as do the things that fortune bestows on us. The most conceited person in the world is the one who has just drawn the first prize in a lottery. I suppose this strangely unsupported self-esteem is itself a survival of primeval demonism; it is vainglory over one's success in having captured the favor of a malicious deity.

However, explain as we will, the deep-seated, unreasoning conviction is there. As I have already admitted, I have it myself, although I may (and timidly do) harbor some doubt concerning the efficacy of the traditional prophylactic. At any rate, touching wood can do no harm; and it is just as well to be on the safe side.

As with superstitions, so it is with antipathies, with prejudices. The habits acquired in overcoming one generic dislike do not always facilitate our conquest of another. A citizen may have developed a fairly open mind with regard to socialism and yet remain in stubborn darkness on the subject of intercollegiate football. An alumnus may accept hospitably all sorts of innovations in admission requirements, while remaining hostile to any change in college music. There are some matters in which we feel discussion to be unavailing, because no amount of discussion, no amount of argument, no amount of evidence could induce us to change our minds. No doubt we can all find in our mansions some windows whose shutters are nailed fast; or, if we cannot find them, our friends can find them for us.

Since I have taken myself as an example in superstition, I may now make confession of an inhibitive prejudice of my own. There is one field of exploration which I will not enter with firm intent to be impartial: that is the domain of phenomena which we call "spiritualistic." The word "psychic" makes me sick; the mention of medium throws my judicial balance out of gear. It is not that I have kept out of the field; again and again I have strayed into it, always to be confronted with the sign, "No trespassing. Police take notice." I have rubbed shoulders with spiritualists and listened to their stories and their professions of faith. I have attended *séances* — at which, to be sure, nothing ever happened. Once I lived for some time in Paris with a noted medium and minister, a man for whom subsequently a great spiritualist temple was erected in America (it is now devoted to moving pictures). I have diligently read thick volume after thick volume, written by devotees and converts, full of authentic testimony to the supernatural. I have sincerely tried to inform myself. Sincerely? Yes, sincerely, but not in due meekness; for all the while, deep down in my consciousness, I have felt the assurance that nothing I might read or hear or see would make the slightest difference. That is my confession. Perhaps everyone could, if this were an experience meeting, contribute an item, or even two or three.

Now, voluntary ignorance of some matters does not imply inability to search into others. Perhaps, indeed.

the shelter of blinders may enable us to look all the more intently along the line in which we wish to see. And yet, can we really see aright in any direction, when we have a blind spot in one eye? All knowledge is so interlocked that a dark patch anywhere in the sky may vitiate our perception — or at any rate, our general estimate — of the whole firmament. Wherever we turn our glass, the shadow of that void pursues us. And our heavens are thickly dotted with such emptinesses.

"All men naturally desire to know." Yes; but, however it may have been with a Greek philosopher, for us un-philosophic moderns the dictum needs amendment. All men, let us say, naturally desire to know those things which are not likely to disturb their vested interests, their cherished beliefs, their satisfying superstitions, their pet antipathies. That is a considerable list of restrictions; and as long as we stick to them, as long as we accept the divine gift of curiosity with such reservations, we shall not be burdened with omniscience. If each man had only one reservation, and all the reservations were different, there might be some prospect of a collective achievement of universal knowledge. But alas! such an ideal distribution of inhibitions is far away from the fact. This or that tabu may affect nearly the entire human race; most of those which I have enumerated belong to vast groups rather than to single individuals. Many a man, no doubt, has all the prejudices ever catalogued, while nobody that we are likely to meet has rid himself of the whole category.

This much comfort we may take to ourselves: every window opened is just so much gain to the opener. It may be also a mite contributed to humanity's quest for know-ledge; but even though it add nothing to the whole col-lection, it will appreciably augment the store of the individual householder. Happily we begin to get our pay in light as soon as we pull up one blind. We are not obliged to wait for our interest until we shall have accumulated a discouraging quota of investment; every deposit brings immediate return. And, though habits may not transfer themselves, we can transfer them, and are likely to do so when we find that a new habit is both possible and profitable. After a while, the free air spirit may come to us, and we can no longer sleep contentedly in a close atmosphere. Just as by repeated indulgence in human weakness we contract a vice, so by one emancipating effort after another we acquire a virtue — the virtue of an open mind.

Every window through which we can see enhances our powers and brings us so much nearer to completeness, whether the outlook be upon science or art or play or duty. Most conspicuously rewarding, however, is an unobstructed view of the works of our fellow-creatures. O to see the thought that lies behind our neighbor's word, the impulse that causes his act! Without such vision we can understand neither him nor ourselves. For men's doings are determined by tangled, hidden motives; men's speech hardly ever succeeds in saying what they really mean. Men are a ceaseless irritation to one another because they are ceaselessly misrepresenting themselves to the eye which sees only the act and to the ear which hears only the word. Throw wide open the window of sympathetic comprehension, and most of the annoyances will vanish: you will behold, not a mob of contrary, selfish brutes, intent on satisfying their stupid desires at other people's expense, but a host of well-meaning, one-eyed fellow-mortals stumbling along like ourselves, knowing no more than we do whither they are bent. They may be compared to a crowd of umbrella-carriers in a gusty storm, clashing, butting, interfering with one another, not because of any hostile intention, but because they cannot see.

Of all the ills that beset us in this life, the most exhausting are those which arise within ourselves. No other creature, no malign fate can inflict on us suffering so acute as that which is self-inflicted. And of our self-imposed penalties the severest is anger — anger, which blinds us to the world and consumes us within. Even a brief attack of it requires a long convalescence; and habitual anger, or hatred, wastes and embitters a whole existence. Now, nearly all anger — I do not say all, because sometimes wrath may be righteous — nearly all anger springs from ignorance. Open in time the eye of reason, and keep it steadfastly open, if the agony is to be avoided. There is no better motto of practical conduct than "put yourself in his place."

Consider the dog who so tries our patience by barking all night: what is he doing, from the cosmic standpoint? He is exercising the virtue of watchfulness, for which we keep him and so highly commend him. The fury engendered by a mouse who gnaws our books may be allayed if we remember that she is dutifully providing for her family. That thought will not restore our books nor solace our sorrow over their loss, but it will mitigate our fury, which hurts us far more than loss or sorrow. The moth, laying her eggs in our best overcoat, is following the blessed instinct of parenthood. The ant, who, despite all lets and hindrances, awakens our indignation by persistently invading our sugar, is bravely earning a livelihood in the face of almost invincible obstacles. Or, turning to our own kind, may we not revise our judgment of the guileful fruit-dealer who has handed us a counterfeit quarter? Certain it is that someone has deceived him even as he has deceived us; and therefore he, even as we shall presently do, is passing on his trouble to another. We are fellows in misfortune and iniquity.

We all crave comfort; and what is more comforting than comradeship, as compared with the isolation of self-satisfied blindness? Let us look out upon the world through unshaded windows, and we shall find it full of fresh interest, full of fascinating problems, full of lives at some point similar to ours, somehow entering into our own circle. And we need never be alone.

Batrachoerpatomachia

BESIDE the Cadillac Trail, between Gorham and Bee-hive, is a round spring, and in the middle of the spring is a stone. On this stone, as I approached, sat a plump, stately frog, who seemed rapt in bland contemplation of the universe. It was only a seeming, though, for as it turned out, he was really on the alert, keeping close watch on a deadly enemy. That foe was a snake, who lay outstretched on the shore in front of the little isle, fixing his intended victim with wicked eyes. Thus Cain looked at Abel. Murder was in the air. In fact, just as I reached the spot, the serpent darted like a streak of lightning; and at the same moment the frog leaped. Neither was in time. The subtil beast did not seize the batrachian by the head, as he had planned; nor did the fugitive escape. The latter had taken a sidelong jump, which carried him almost clear — all but one of his hind feet, which remained in the pur-suer's mouth. Then the battle began.

The frog, as I have hinted, was a big one. I shall not say how big; it is hard to be truthful in stating the di-mensions of a frog. Everyone knows the story of the frogs in South America. A frog, like a fish, grows as it recedes into the past. Anyhow, it was a big frog. The snake, a reptile of the type popularly known as "striped adder," was of moderate length. Snakes, too, have a strange facility of elongation in retrospect, but their dimensions offer less difficulty to a veracious recorder, because they can be stated in terms of linear measure. I should say that this snake was two and a half feet long.

Snakes have very bad table manners. They attempt mouthfuls that would excite the envy of the most expeditious frequenter of the Waldorf. A snake, you see, takes his whole meal in one gulp. How many a boy would give his boots to be able to do that trick! Often a snake will tackle a mouthful that looks bigger than himself; and, as far as I know, he always gets away with it. Once, in the middle of a road, I came across a pretty little green snake, who, for reasons best known to himself, had come to that public place to make his meal. His luncheon, which he held headfirst in his mouth, was a middle-sized frog, also green. Perhaps the harmony of color had first kindled the concupiscence of the hunter and made him yearn that two hearts should beat as one. At any rate, there he was, with the frog's head in his mouth, which, of course, had to be pretty wide open. Snakes do not appear to the best advantage when their mouths are open wide. They have a singularly disagreeable smile. It is not one of the "smiles that makes you happy." Smiling is all right in the right place — I try to assume a cheerful disposition, myself; but I protest it is not good form to smile when you are swallowing a live green frog.

The best place to study table manners is at sea. I recall, in particular, one old tub of a ship, part steamer and part sailing vessel. We were bound from London to New York. There were a good many passengers, and I could guess just why they had taken that boat rather than another; they had taken it for the same reason that I had. Still, old as she might be, I had confidence she was safe; for the rats had not forsaken her. One night I awoke with a sociable rodent perched on my hand. But he did not tarry long. Another, doubtless a more *blasé* friend of his, used to make more extended calls. He would drop in pretty regularly just before I retired. Usually he had nothing of moment to communicate, contenting himself with a rat's substitute for small talk; on one visit, however, he evidently had something especial on his mind. First he peeped out, to make sure I was there. Then, withdrawing to his residence, he pulled forth a captain's biscuit and drew it to the middle of the floor, where he dropped it and sat looking up at me with a superior air. When he thought me sufficiently impressed, he dragged it back again and disappeared. I was considerably relieved to learn that the rats could find something good to eat on that ship. There is no telling what a hungry rat may do.

I wonder why it is, by the way, that we have such a horror of rats and mice — all the "gent trotte-menu," as La Fontaine prettily calls them. They are intelligent creatures, and in various ways deserving of admiration, mice for their beauty, rats for their domestic virtues. To be sure, they do like to destroy things which we prize, comestibles and books, our bodily and mental food. That, I conceive, is a sufficient reason for wanting to get rid of them, but not for the shudder which they provoke. Really there is nothing uncanny about a rat, except perhaps its ingenuity. In one country house which I shared for a season with a rat settlement, the rodents had developed such aldermanic proportions that every ghostly association was outgrown. Portly and unafraid, they went about their business like real City Fathers, with no more secrecy than piano movers; they had actually made, for convenience' sake, neat little paths through the grass between my cottage and the next, and one could see them, in broad daylight, cheerfully and corpulently waddling their way to and fro. The arts of duplicity and concealment were left to us, poor human vermin, who watched and strained to snatch a bare subsistence from the monopoly of the overlords. Who knows? Perhaps they regarded us as ghoulish nocturnal prowlers, and shuddered when they met us.

Now, when it comes to serpents, a moderate shiver is permissible. To see a live beast move so fast over land, without any feet, is enough to upset anybody. . Remember how terrified horses were at their first sight of automobiles. Yet I wonder how much of our fear is instinctive, and how much acquired. When I was a very little child (so my mother has told me), I used to pick up small snakes, bring them into our home, and deposit them on the carpet, with the comment, "pretty" — to the wild consternation of the household. Nowadays, to lift up a serpent in my hand requires all the strength of will that I possess; I sometimes do it, to prove to myself that I can, but the creepiness of it cannot be overcome. This immoderate repugnance, in a region where snakes are harmless, may be in part an inheritance from other times and climes, but in the main it must be derived from gruesome snake stories, the gruesomest of all being the one in Genesis. Yes, I am sure the Bible is responsible for a good half of our antipathy, and for nearly all our sense of righteousness in that hatred. Every normal boy over six and every normal man under sixty believes that to kill a snake is always justifiable; nay, more, that not to kill a snake, when the opportunity comes, is to fail in one's manifest duty. Would you leave poor old Adam unavenged? Impenitent the subtil beasts are, and vicious, as one can see from their impudent fashion of sticking out their tongues.

To the Bible we may attribute also the prevalence, though not the origin, of the strange notion that serpents have stings in their tails, like dragons and scorpions. Once, at a railway crossing in Jamaica Plain, a dainty little green snake had strayed upon the track, and a lady, suddenly espying it at her feet, uttered a scream of fright. Gallantly rushed to her rescue a huge policeman, drawing his trusty night-stick as he ran. At his first onslaught, the cunning criminal contrived to ensconce itself in a groove beside a rail, where the battering of the legal club could not quite reach it. Nothing daunted, the club pounded away, its blows descending now on one side, now on the other, of the ambushed culprit. The guardian of the law grew red in the face as his violent exercise continued. A crowd gathered, tense with excitement. Still the steady hammering went on, and still the guilty one lay unscathed. Fearless determination sat on the policeman's brow, while his powerful strokes increased rather than diminished their thickness and fastness. What the outcome of the combat might have been, no one will ever know, had not some miscreant on the outer fringe of the assembly shrilly ejaculated: "Look out for his stinger!" The ruddy face turned pale, and beads of sweat exuded from the blanched forehead; the mighty arm faltered, the ponderous body recoiled. And the sly little sinner took advantage of the moment to slip from sight.

Had the object of the bystander's outcry been a different kind of creature, there might have been wisdom in his warning. I can remember a day when my cousin and I, as boys, took a swim in Lake Quinsigamond, having carelessly thrown our clothing on the shore. It was a pretty little beach; now close to the crowded bridge that leads to the White City, it was then secluded and remote. On our return from our aqueous adventure, we sought out our clothes and found them, to be sure, on the spot where we had left them; but that spot, as we discovered to our dismay, was occupied also by a hornets' nest, on which our garments reposed; and hornets in considerable numbers were reposing on them. We were miles from home. No barrels were near. Our clothes must be had. The occasion called for serpentine craft, and no serpent was craftier than we. Searching along the shore, we found two very long sapling trunks which had apparently been used as fishing-rods. Armed with these appliances, we stole upon our objective, and halted as far off as the rods could reach. Each separate article was then fished forth at the end of a rod, shaken violently in the air, and tossed afar. Afterwards, when the tumult had subsided, we proceeded to collect our disjected integuments, and, after cautious examination, to put them on. And we escaped without a sting.

Another perilous situation comes back to me. This time I was alone. It was on Blue Hill, in the State of Maine. The height of Blue Hill was reckoned to be 996 feet, but local pride, erecting a four-foot pile of stones on its peak, had raised the altitude to an even thousand. On the apex of this rather shaky structure I was standing, with folded arms, wondering what Napoleon would have thought about, if, instead of being at the bottom of the pyramid, he had been at the top, where the forty centuries were. As I meditated, I was dreamily aware of an eagle circling above me. Suddenly I awoke from my dream. There could be no doubt about it. Like the swings of the razor-edged pendulum in Edgar Poe's pit, the eagle's revolutions were diminishing in compass and swiftly approaching. Almost before I had reached this conclusion, he was swooping to earth, directly over my head. There was no time to scramble down from my rickety perch.

All the stories I had ever read, all the pictures I had ever
seen, of sweet babes or innocent lambs carried off in the
cruel talons of a bird of prey, rushed unbidden into my
mind. But I remembered also what I had read of the
power of the human eye. As the eagle drew near, I gazed
at him as fixedly as my unstable footing permitted. The
Monarch of the Air paused for a moment amazed, cowed,
uncertain, then, with a raucous cry, retreating, vanished
among the trees. I have told this incident to several of
my friends, but have never yet found one who would believe it. Anyhow, it is true. Perhaps it will receive credence from someone who does not know me so well.

I wish I knew more about birds. I should like to be
able to call each species by name and to recognize each
by its song. What a satisfaction it would be to go out in
the morning with a little note-book, wherein to jot down
a record of every ornithological specimen I saw or heard;
and then to spend the rest of the day reciting the list to
all comers! Bird-lovers always appear so happy! In fact,
their happiness would seem even to transcend the unhap-
piness they cause others. Of that sorrow they are bliss-
fully unaware, just as the blessed souls in Heaven have
no vexatious cognizance of the sufferings of the damned.
Once, on a bicycle, I was passing by a pond in Waltham.
It was spring, and the air was alive with shrill chirping.
On the road was halted an automobile containing four
bird-sharks. One was turning over the pages of a bird-
volume, one stood at attention with pencil and bird-
record-book, while two were eagerly scanning the trees
with bird-glasses. Impatience, surprise, and disappointment were registered by all four faces. Why, O ye knowing ones, why? Ignorant as I am, I could have told them
that even the eyes of Argus would find nothing in that

foliage; for the multitudinous chirping which seemed to fill the whole atmosphere came from no trees, but from the ventriloquous throats of countless gay little frogs who peopled the pond.

How did the blithe little devils ever learn the trick? The pipe of the baby frog is the most innocently cheerful song I know; it comes with the very first flowers, the first soft breezes, and it gladdens the heart with confidence. Yet it is full of guile. When you approach, it stops, leaving a silence profound and full of mystery. But its resumption is even more mysterious. For the life of you, you cannot tell from what direction it comes. There was one road in the hill country of North Carolina over which I walked again and again; and every time I passed, I could have sworn (had I been a swearing man) that the deafening warble was bursting from the very ground under my feet. Do the froglets learn the art at their grandmother's knee, or do they get it instinctively, without study? Was the First Frog created with it, or did some batrachian wizard invent it and pass it on to his progeny? And if it was thus bequeathed, was not the testament illegal, according to the statute prohibiting the inheritance of acquired characters?

In pedagogical criminology, the statute is adapted to human society, and applies to acquired habits. It reads: acquired habits are not automatically transferred; that is, skill gained in one pursuit is not necessarily of any assistance in a different one. But I cannot help thinking that this law, like Weismann's (and some others), is subject to occasional infraction. At any rate, a dog who has acquired the habit of barking at automobiles readily transfers that habit to bicycles and even to pedestrians. And I believe he does it automatically; at least, that is the most charitable supposition. I once saw a big dog plunging out furiously at a passing car, and, as I watched him, his gait looked peculiar. The reason for this eccentricity became clear when he returned from his latrating orgy: he had only three legs. Instantly his past and his future were revealed. On one of these attempted highway holdups he had lost a limb. Nevertheless he would continue his mad practice until, with the loss of another leg, he should perforce abandon his acquired habit.

One of my acquired habits is a secret terror of dogs. I like them, and they seem to like me, but they give me something of the shrinking sensation that most people get from a snake. In my aversion to snakes there is a large element of the unknown, whereas I can account perfectly for my fear of our canine friend. When I was about three years old, a dog, which I was stooping to caress, snapped crossly and bit me through the lip. It is hard to regain confidence in a trusted chum who turns and bites you through the lip. The moral shock is far severer than the physical, although the latter is bad enough.

In wolves I have never put faith, and therefore have never suffered disappointment; besides, all the wolves I have known have been safely caged. Consequently, they inspire me with no horror, plague though they be to the folds. *Triste lupus stabulis:* that reminds me of a certain elderly man, evidently a stranger, whom I met near Tufts College. He was surveying the pleasant campus as I came along. "Is that a college?" he inquired. "I never went to college," he continued, regretfully, when I had answered his question. "I went all through the high school, but I could n't never go to college; and I 've always been sorry. I had Latin down through Virgil. There was one thing happened once in the Latin class

that I could n't never understand. I had to translate a
Latin sentence, *Triste lupus stabulis;* and I translated it,
'a sad wolf in the stable.' And I ain't never been able to
see why everybody laughed so. I've thought of it many
and many a time, but I ain't never dared to speak of it to
nobody till now. Perhaps if I'd gone to college, I could
have understood it." I left him still gazing wistfully at
the college walls.

No wolf, sad or merry, ever invaded the stables of my
Lombard dairyman. Him I came across in a train from
Rome to Naples, a man of fifty or so, on his way south to
buy some cattle. He was from a place north of Milan —
Monza, I think. Although he easily understood Italian,
he spoke his local dialect, which, however, I was able,
after a little practice, to follow. Good stocks they had in
the south, he averred, and good grazing, but the people
had no enterprise and let everything go to waste; a company of northerners ought to be organized to exploit the
unused resources of that country. He himself belonged
to a very prosperous concern, which shipped butter and
cheese even to Spain; and he pulled out of his pocket a
package of orders, to show me. All the members were of
one family: sixty-eight of them, four generations, who
worked the same great farm and once a month all dined
at the same long table. The head of the firm was his
grandmother, now ninety-two, who had charge of all the
moneys; when she should die, the company would probably go to pieces, for it was her will, her authority, which
held them all together. We became such good friends that
he offered to supply me with milk, free of charge, as long
as he and I should be in Naples — an invitation whose
sincerity was beyond doubt, although I was unable to
accept it. His cows, he said, were good ones; they aver-

aged ten quarts a day. And when he proceeded to ask me
about American cows, and I (wishing to be moderate)
mentioned twenty quarts, he assured me, with a polite
smile, that I must be mistaken, for no cow had been
known to give more than twelve. I let it go at that. Not
for the world would I have introduced a noxious germ of
dissatisfaction between a cattleman — especially so generous a one — and his own cow.

> Hanc ego præstolor manibus mulgere paratis,
> Hac implebo decem missurus vascula Mopso.

Surely it would ill become Mopsus to criticize.

But I started out, it seems to me, to tell a wild-animal
story, and all my animals have grown as tame as if they
had listened to the strains of Orpheus' lyre.

What was the sylvan beast? It can hardly have been
my first marmot, which, just above the snow-line in the
Selkirks, startled my unaccustomed ears with its musical,
mysterious, burglar-like whistle.

Nor can it have been my porcupine, the sociable one.
It was in the wilderness of the Canadian National Park
that I came across him. I had put up at Emerald Lake,
and was out alone on the way to Ta-kak-kaw Falls, whose
roar could be heard miles away. Face to face in the trail
we unexpectedly met, the porcupine more astonished than
I; for I warrant he had never before seen a man, whereas I
had seen a good many porcupines. This one bristled a bit,
from excitement no doubt; but he did not turn his back;
he showed neither hostility nor fear. Instead, he stood
there at my feet, peering curiously up at me, while I
stared down at him. As the prolonged silence became embarrassing, I picked up a little stick and began to scratch
his back. Whereat he gently arched it, and grunted con-

tentedly, like a pig. I think that is the only word I ever elicited from a porcupine.

Equally innocent of contact with humanity must have been another animal whose acquaintance I made nearer home. Do not rejoice prematurely: it was not the kind of animal you think. With a friend, I was strolling over the stony beach, on a secluded piece of the Maine coast, when, ahead, we saw something strange. A shapeless mass of moving matter, twice as big as a man's head, came bumping and tumbling along over the stones. It advanced fast, though evidently with painful effort. I never saw anything so weird. When it reached a point about ten or twelve feet from us, it stopped. Then we saw that it was a huge hunk of fish borne and hauled by a mink. Becoming suddenly aware of our presence, the little carrier laid down his burden and approached. We stood perfectly still. He came briskly up to us, sniffed at our toes, looked searchingly up into our faces; then, apparently convinced that we were harmless, went back to his fish and resumed his journey. I hope he enjoyed his meal; for myself, I do not care much for fish.

Speaking of sea food, do you know the Maine recipe for cooking coot? You take two of the fowls, two flatirons, and a kettle of water. Put the coot into the kettle, put the kettle on the fire, put the lid on the kettle, and the two flatirons on the lid, to hold it down. Let it boil for six hours. Then open the kettle, throw away the birds, and eat the flatirons.

Now I remember. The story I set out to tell had to do with eating; and I believe it had a herpato-batrachian flavor. Once, when I was a small boy, walking in a field, I nearly stepped on a fairly long speckled adder of amazing fatness. I was at an age when, as I have said, it is deemed obligatory always to kill or molest a snake. Accordingly I picked up a big stone — a "rock," we should have called it. By the way, I recently heard a neighbor's wife in Maine telling of two bad boys whom she had seen "rockin' a cow." But let us leave the cow to her slumbers, and return to our snake. They are horribly elusive creatures! Being at close range, however, I hit the reptile with my stone. The victim winced, but did not budge. I rightly guessed that it was hampered by corpulence; but I did not guess all. A second rock, flung with some force, reached its mark; whereupon the serpent unceremoniously belched up a great toad. The toad hopped away unconcernedly, and the speckled adder fled.

It all comes back to me now. A long way behind, I left a little green snake on the point of devouring a green frog, which it was holding by the snout in the middle of a road. This time I was not a life-saver — only a spectator. In fact, my rôle in the ensuing scene is negligible. Finding a favorable spot, the serpent began the strenuous task of getting outside the frog. Wider and wider its jaws parted, as it worked itself, little by little, up over the party of the second part. It was a slow operation, and manifestly painful to the operator. At last all was engulfed but two hind feet, which still for some time awkwardly protruded. But with strength restored by a good rest, Comestor wrestled again with his meal, and succeeded in sinking the encumbrances out of sight. Then he fatly slid to the roadside and vanished in the grass.

However, we are not yet done. There is more unfinished business — the business of the other snake and the other frog. Let me remind you. This frog, a powerful one, from his perch on a stone in the middle of a spring, jumped as the aggressor darted; and the attacking party grabbed him by the left hind foot, instead of by the nose, as he had intended. Then began the Homeric contest which lent its name to this chronicle. It lasted twenty minutes: I know, for I held the watch.

As the battle went on, the striped adder gradually climbed its enveloping course up the batrachian's leg, until it reached the top; then it could go no further. Meanwhile there was a lashing and splashing, the snake laboring to pull the frog out of the spring, and vainly reaching with its tail for something to hold to; the frog trying to keep the snake under water long enough to drown him. At one time, the serpent would weary, his grip on the leg would relax, his jaws would slip down a quarter of an inch, half an inch, even an inch; then a fresh effort would send them up again to their former hold. Blood trickled out of the corners of his mouth; at first I thought it came from the frog's leg, but later I concluded it was from the throat of the snake. At other moments, the frog would tire, he would cease pulling his wrigglesome adversary down, he would even turn on his back and float helplessly, whereupon he would be pulled almost to the edge, and I believed all was over; but miraculously he revived, struck out once more, and towed his slippery antagonist into the middle.

The fortunes of war were evenly divided; the protecting deities seemed equally potent, or equally impotent. The seesaw ended in a deadlock, both combatants exhausted, both apparently put to sleep, with the leg of the one still in the mouth of the other. After counting ten quite slowly, I pulled the snake off and tossed him ashore, where he lay, stiff as a stick, with his mouth wide open.

The frog, however, directly he was released, clambered nimbly on his stone, puffed himself out, and glanced triumphantly around, as if to say: "Gee, fellers! Just look at what I done to that snake!"

And the author, on his own behalf, echoes that exclamation.

Imagination and the Lack of it

"IT will be a fine city when it's finished" was, according to tradition, the intelligent Englishman's judgment on New York. "What a beautiful church it would be, if it were not so cluttered up!" said a young American architect when he first stepped inside Westminster Abbey. And the Eternal City: what is it but an eternity of clutter and making over? I suppose that is why so many people are bitterly disappointed in Rome. Things so completely overlap — one ruin built out of the stuff of another — that nothing can be reconstructed in imagination. One sees the process of change, either active or fossilized, but one cannot guess what anything has changed from or to. Only the early churches, St. Clement, St. Lawrence, St. Agnes, make a clear appeal to the mind's eye. Of course I say nothing of those monstrosities which, in the last few years, have come to rob the metropolis of the dented dignity that was left her; when one thinks of them, one can only pray for an earthquake. No; to get a view of genuine Roman ruins, one must go afar, to Verona, to Orange, to Nîmes, even to Paris.

Likewise, *mutatis mutandis*, has fared the university town of Cambridge in Massachusetts. Now on its rapid way from big villagedom to the status of a citified suburb, it presents to the callous observer nothing but the unattractive symptoms of shift. However, if one be disposed to repine because nothing beautiful goes up, one may be consoled by the reflection that there is nothing of transcendent loveliness to come down. To be sure, in lieu of real beauty there is a certain sedateness here and there in some of the perishing structures, a certain savor of old New England, occasionally a precious association that one relinquishes unwillingly.

For instance, on Kirkland St., there stood until yesterday the plain but inviting mansion, earnest and spacious, planned by Charles W. Eliot at the time of his first marriage. It was a double house — half for his parents, who had lost the greater part of their fortune, half for himself and his bride. This latter part ultimately fell to the lot of Miss Grace Norton, sister of Charles Eliot Norton and cousin of Charles Eliot, a dear spirit who combined to a rare degree the love of books and the love of living people. An authority on Montaigne, a delver into the curious lore of all the ages, a devourer, too, of the latest tomes (in her nineties she was reading Amy Lowell's *Keats* and Wheeler's monumental treatise on insects), she had all her brother's fine gift for friendship. In that house she dwelt for many years; and there she died, within a few months of the death of her famous cousin. They were, indeed, almost exactly of an age; until his last year, he always paid her a visit on her birthday.

Like her cousin, Miss Norton was intensely interested in human character, and curious of all its manifestations. Inevitably, then, she was impelled to study her dwelling for bits of evidence of the spiritual make-up of her relative, the builder. A design carefully thought out and unswervingly executed: that was her general verdict. Yet there was one detail that disturbed and puzzled her. At the head of the main stairway lay the passage from one room to another; and to make the crossing one had to take a step down and another step up, the landing's level being eight inches or so beneath that of the upper entry. Here was a problem: however could so careful, so clever a man have introduced this needless inconvenience? Every day she suffered the inconvenience; every day the problem posed itself anew. Once, when he was calling on her, she asked him. His answer, with a laugh, was: "Sheer ignorance."

This response satisfied Miss Norton only for the moment. If her cousin was so ignorant of construction, why had his lack of experience shown itself here and nowhere else? What was there in this particular spot that had exposed a weakness in the contriver? And what was that weakness? No, the solution was wrong; he must try again. Many years afterward, therefore, she reminded him of the circumstance. Once more she pointed out the senseless depression between room and room. She repeated her query and his response. "Would you give the same reason now?" she inquired. He reflected a moment. "No," he replied, "my answer now would be: lack of imagination."

Lack of imagination — the want that turns us into automata, that makes us do things merely because other people do them. In the case under discussion, hoary precedent had decreed the unnecessary descent between entry and room, and imagination had failed to span it. Why such a hiatus had ever become customary, I can only conjecture. Perhaps people planned and built their houses in sections. Thomas Jefferson is said to have left out entirely the stairway from his design for Monticello, his stately residence, and to have discovered the omission too late to make any fit provision for communication between floor and floor. Many ancient houses, both here and in the old country, abound in mysterious changes of level, which, when passages are dark, are conducive to impromptu acrobatics. This peculiarity is purposely reproduced in some very recent structures, patterned in imitation of the now fashionable "colonial" style. Thus, in the delightful Princeton Inn, we slide down a sharp declivity in the corridor to our electrically lighted and steam-heated rooms. To match the interior, the outside is given a "primitive" appearance by the projection of every fourth or fifth brick beyond the vertical plane of its mates. The general effect is not bad, if partially veiled by creeping verdure. At any rate, it has a justification which cannot be claimed by the grotesque absurdities which go under the name of "primitive" in the "advanced" art circles of our day.

All this, though, has nothing to do with President Eliot and his home; for he, surely, was following no fad. The extraordinary feature of the story is that a leader of men, respected and renowned for his foresight, his vision, should have found himself lacking in imagination. To be sure, he was young when he built the house, and presumably had done little or nothing in that line before. On the other hand, before he was thirty-five he had new and far-reaching views on education, although his own work as an educator had necessarily been of the smallest scope. All his life long he was a seer. So was Emerson, who still communed with the gods in their own language when he could no longer recall the terrestrial name for an umbrella. The fact is, everybody lacks imagination, as well as memory, in certain quarters. The difference between genius and dunce is that the former is unimaginative in streaks, the latter in continuity.

I used to think that women, as compared with men, were unimaginative. Now I am distrustful of all such generalizations. Yet my evidence was good as far as it went. A woman, when she lays an object down (a plate, for instance), will leave it projecting an inch, or even several inches, beyond the edge of the table, in such fashion that the passer-by, brushing against it, will be in peril of knocking it off — a proof that the feminine mind, at the moment of depositing, is incapable of picturing the subsequent history of the deposit. This shortcoming, however, pales into pettiness beside the crime of hiding the matches.

Hiding the matches, like stealing corpses from the gallows, is a misdeed that belongs to the past, matches in our day being of use only to smokers, who generally keep a supply of them about their persons. But there was a time, remembered by some of us, when houses were lighted in the city by gas, in the country by lamps; and that was the heyday of the match. Now imagine (if you are a man) or try to imagine (if you are a woman) the situation at the moment when a person (usually a man) enters a dark room and wishes to strike a light. If the room were not dark, the light would not be needed. Inevitable, then, is this combination: darkness and need of a flame. In other words, the seeker for a match cannot be guided by his eyes. He reaches blindly for the nearest corner of the mantelpiece, where the matches ought to be. But they are not. After a thorough tactile investigation of the obvious corner, he goes cautiously groping along the shelf, upsetting glass vases and porcelain shepherdesses, until he reaches the clock. Remembering that he once found the runaways tucked in the rear of that timepiece, he thrusts his fingers behind. Nothing but dust. Then he progresses from ornament to ornament along the other side. The upshot only too often is that he has to go downstairs to a room already gassed, ere he can carry the divine fire to the chamber of his choice. Then he discovers the matches grinning at him maliciously from a brand-new vantage-point on the whatnot.

This looks like a petty vexation. So is a drip of water; yet the stone can tell what dripping drops can do if they keep a-dripping and a-dropping persistently enough. The truth is, the practice of concealing matches was the most ruthless homewrecker we had until the advent of Freud. Hidden Matches were the Suppressed Desires of the Victorian era.

But why did they do it? Let us attempt a bit of psychoanalysis. Those were the days when "the place of woman was in the home." The home was her dominion and her pride; the dominant purpose of her life, next to looking better than other women, was to make her home look better than other women's homes. Now, in the adornment of her home, as in the adornment of her person, the fundamental principle (how changed it is now!) was to keep the really useful articles out of sight. Even among such unconcealable furnishings as chairs, the more sittable ones were relegated to the background. And matches — homely, unesthetic, utilitarian matches — were doomed to invisibility. This, you must remember, was in the daytime. That is the crux of the whole matter; the room was always put to rights by day. Day, when the blessed sunshine reveals to the illumined seeker every secret recess. How was a creature destitute of imagination to conceive how it would be in the dark? And darkness, as I have said, was the indispensable prerequisite of every match-hunting enterprise.

The argument appears conclusive; yet it has a flaw. We have proved beyond a peradventure that woman is lacking in imagination. But have we proved that man is not? How do we know that the male, if the household cares devolved upon him, would be less secretive of matches than the female? How can we tell whether the supposed difference is functional or organic? We know nothing more about it than did those medieval theologians who solemnly argued that women were not human beings — *feminas homines non esse.*

How shall we test them? Suppose we observe them at a summer resort, where both sexes have betaken themselves ostensibly for a change. In both we observe the same absence of adaptation to a new environment. Both are obstinately bent on doing exactly the same things they do at home, and, as far as possible, in exactly the same way — just as a spider, wherever you put her, will spin precisely the same web. Mountains may offer their mystery, woods their wildness, oceans may sing their siren song: all to no purpose; not an eye will be lifted to the crown. Golf, tennis, motor-cars, teas, dinners, dances make *rus* a replica of *urbs*. And between man and woman there is little to choose. The one inclines more to golf, the other to tea; that is all. Set them down in Florida, in Maine, on the French Riviera: it is always the same, it is simply New York wheeled to another spot. Why, then, have these people ever left the "little old" metropolis? Because other people do; and these other people are following others still. And none of them have imagination enough to conceive of anything different.

But stay! here is perhaps an exception. Behold an adventurous little band that breaks out into a picnic. It has all the equipment that a picnic should have. Hampers are filled with the edibles that regale a hotel-dweller. Thermos bottles are ready to disgorge hot soup and hot coffee.

Despite thermos, though, they must have a fire. To be sure, it is a beastly hot day, and the smoke always blows into one's eyes; they have nothing to cook; fires are forbidden. It is an abnormally dry season, too, when one loose spark may devastate a whole countryside. Nevertheless, a fire they must have. Why? Because people always have fires at picnics; a picnic cannot be imagined without one.

At a hotel in Nice, at luncheon-time, I have seen a company of my countrymen raising a loud and piteous wail because they could not get dry Martini cocktails. Surrounded as they were by all the gifts of the vine, they could not be consoled for the lack of the one drink they always drank at home. "Remote, unfriended, melancholy, slow" — such is a Martiniless meal, a refection introduced by a mere alien *apéritif*. From all their travels they resolutely excluded, as far as in them lay, all that was foreign.

Why is a dunce a dunce? By "dunce" I mean a human being destitute of that most human of traits, imagination. The dunce stands somewhere between *homo sapiens* and the other primates. But for imagination, man had never been; there would have been no evolution — nothing but fundamentalism. Now, I suppose a dunce is a dunce chiefly because he is born a dunce. We all have our changeless spots. Yet it is not entirely a matter of birth: education has much to do with it. Our schooling may teach us how to earn a living, how to read and cipher, how to vote; but if it does not develop in us the power of seeing beyond the here and now, it is not up to the standard of *homo sapiens*. And I suspect that much of our pedagogy falls short in just that respect. It fails to cultivate awareness of the unknown, the sense of mystery and the quenchless curiosity which it engenders. It makes a pretty top, but goes no deeper.

When I was in Paris in my boyhood, there came frequently to the house where I lived a very beautiful South American lady, dainty, talkative, good-natured, somewhere in her middle twenties, married (although I cannot recall ever having seen her husband). She played the piano; she spoke French like a Frenchwoman born; in dress and manners she was elegance personified. As might be expected, she was fond of the shops; and every now and then she would ask me to act as her escort on her shopping expeditions. Why she wanted me passed my comprehension. I liked it well enough; her company was pleasant and she generally bought me a sweet. But what on earth did I contribute? A child of twelve could hardly serve as a cavalier; moreover, I was shy and by no means forthputting. There were no packages to carry. Why was I invited? At last it dawned upon me. I was needed, to interpret the signs on the buildings and the labels on the goods. For the beautiful Spanish lady could not read.

I wonder how far the Señora was — not typical, but symbolical, of American education, in the northern hemisphere as in the southern. How generally do we content ourselves with cultivation of the surface, leaving the subsoil unstirred? And what connection may there be between such shallowness and the prevalent lack of imagination?

Confessio Dantis

IN the divine poem of sin and salvation, "non dopo molte carte", is an episode that has long puzzled me; and the interpretation, as it has at last come to my mind, whether true or false, makes rather a long story. It has to do with the function of the *Comedy*, as contrasted with the *New Life* and the *Banquet;* the gist of it is revelation of character through self-criticism. But first let us look at the troublesome passage, lines 70 to 81 of the third canto of Part I. Dante, guided by Virgil, is approaching the underground river Acheron, which separates the outer court of the nether world from Hell itself.

> When I began to cast my eyes ahead,
>   I saw a crowd beside a river's rim,
>   And, "Master, grant me now to know," I said,
> "Who all these people are.   To cross the brim
>   Of this great water, why do they press on,
>   As I discern amid the twilight dim?"
> And he to me: "When we have further gone,
>   Thou shalt be told, the while our steps we stay
>   Upon the sorry shore of Acheron."
> With lowered eyes, ashamed and in dismay
>   Lest I had him offended, till we came
>   Unto the river, nothing did I say.
>   *Inf.*, III, 70–81.

In Dante's question the casual reader detects nothing indiscreet; nor does he catch the note of rebuke which Dante evidently heard in Virgil's answer. Yet indiscretion and rebuke are here, awakening shame and dismay.

When the poet conceived the scene, he must have put sternness into his master's face, sternness into his voice. Why? What, in his own mental picture, was the reprehensible feature of his own conduct? Of what characteristic fault did he feel himself to be guilty? The voice of Virgil is the voice of Reason, for Reason is Virgil's allegorical rôle. What irrationality has Dante committed? There is only one answer. It must be, his offense is impatience to reach a conclusion before assuring himself of the premises; and he must have regarded this weakness as habitual, this occurrence as symptomatic; else the whole incident were pointless.

The idea of shortcoming and consequent reproof is in the author's mind so clear, so inevitable, that he does not feel the need of explicitly conveying it. This is not the only time. Of the failure to express implied reprobation, we have a striking instance in the scene which depicts the two poets on the point of descending into the pit on the back of the great dragon, Geryon, symbol of Fraud. Dante, who has been parleying with the usurers on the brink of the abyss, on his return finds Virgil already mounted.

> Virgil I found, already climbed along
>   The crupper of the baleful-looking brute.
>   He shouted to me: "Now be brave and strong!
> Down such a stairway now are we to shoot.
>   Climb up in front, for I will sit between
>   To shield thee from the writhing tail acute."
> Like one who has the fever's chill so keen
>   And close at hand, his nails are white with cold,
>   And shivers when a shadow he has seen,
> E'en such was I, hearing what I was told;
>   But none the less his threats had stirred my shame,
>   Which makes a kindly master's servant bold.
>   *Inf.*, xvii, 79–90.

"Threats," *minacce*, is what the text says; yet in Virgil's words it is hard to see any suggestion of threatening:

> "Now be brave and strong!
> Down such a stairway now are we to shoot.
> Climb up in front, for I will sit between
> To shield thee from the writhing tail acute."

There is the notion of danger from the scorpionlike tail, but no hint of menace on Virgil's part — only promise of protection. Here again, in Dante's visualization of the picture, there must have been more than he transferred to his verse; a menacing tone, no doubt, and a threatening shake of the finger.

Another speech of the master contains a gentle reproof so covertly implied that one would never suspect its existence, were it not for the pupil's eagerness to justify himself. This time they are in the vast cemetery where, in fiery tombs, are interred the souls of heretics. Dante's inquiry, whether any of the inmates may be seen, receives this answer:

> "As to thy spoken question, on the spot,
>   Of further craving thou shalt soon be rid;
>   E'en so with the desire thou speakest not."
> "Dear guide," said I, "if I my heart have hid,
>   'T is but to check my speech; and more than once
>   Hast thou my tongue to moderation bid."
>   *Inf.*, x, 16–21.

One does not readily think of Dante as loose-talking — nor as loose-thinking, either. But we must remember, in the first place, what a severe critic he was, of others and of himself; and, next, who was his master in dialectics: that unapproachable expert in mathematical conciseness and precision, St. Thomas Aquinas. Compared to him, any other logician might well think himself slipshod.

Dante, then, with such a model, and with an impulsive temperament, was rightly conscious of a tendency to jump at conclusions; and, having it on his conscience, he confessed it in the *Comedy*.

For the *Comedy* is a book of confession. We often speak of the *New Life*, the *Banquet*, and the *Comedy*, as a series, a trilogy; and there is no harm in so doing, if we remember that the purpose of the third member is quite different from that of the other two. The earlier works are apologies, attempts at justification of the author's life; in the third, sophistry is thrown aside, and fault is freely admitted.

The *New Life*, by idealization, justifies the author's youthful career, and gives it a beautiful though fictitious unity under the dominance of Beatrice. Those girls for whom, in boyhood, Dante wrote verses, appear as a pretty screen, employed to conceal his real devotion to his one and only lady. That love passage, after Beatrice's death, with the sympathetic young person at the window — evidently an affair of considerable moment in the poet's life — is reduced to a passing fancy that ends promptly in the complete triumph of his queen. To be sure, we find, in the descriptions of his grief over his lost love, an occasional note that startles us with a suggestion of morbidness — a note of shame, of abasement, of desire to escape from the sight of men, of conviction that he is an object of contempt — something that makes us wonder whether in his sorrow there can be a sense of guilt. With this something, we may perhaps associate that mysterious sonnet addressed to Dante by his friend Cavalcanti, "Daily I come to seek thee countless times." Few, however, and easily forgotten are such jarring notes. The *New Life* is a symphony of youth quickened by the influence of an angel-lady.

Like to the *New Life* in purpose, but quite different in method, is the *Banquet*. This, too, is a work of justification; its author tells us that the object of the two books is the same, although the tone of the one is boyish, that of the other, mature. The window-girl's domination is not denied or minimized; rather is it, one would judge, exaggerated. But she becomes a symbol. The poet's passion for her is transformed into a passionate quest for knowledge. She is Lady Philosophy. If the *New Life* is justification by idealism, the *Banquet* is justification by allegory. It might be called "The Triumph of Science."

After the two apologies — long after, in my thinking — comes the confession. It is a real confession, signed, in the middle, with the author's name. Good is confessed as well as bad: repentance, solid faith, overpowering love of God and of God's universe, trust in the ultimate salvation of the world and of the poet himself. Furthermore, his last earthly hope — hope that his great poem may yet soften the hearts of the Florentines and move them to call him back and crown him with bay — this final hope, perhaps confided to none other, he here avows:

> If fate decree that e'er my sacred song
>> Where earth and heaven have all their story told,
>> Keeping me lean this many a winter long,
> Shall melt the ire that hath my pretty fold
>> Denied me, where a lamb I laid me down,
>> Hateful to wolves in depredation bold, —
> Mature in voice, mature in fleecy gown,
>> I shall return a poet, shall receive
>> At my baptismal font the laurel crown.
>> *Par.*, xxv, 1–9.

And he declares to us also his world-hope, his expectation of the revival of Imperial power and the restoration of peace to bleeding Italy by that brilliant young leader,

Can Grande della Scala, whom he has seen a boy during the early years of his exile, when he found refuge in Verona. Thus runs the prophecy which the poet puts into the mouth of his own great-great-grandfather, Cacciaguida, in the Heaven of Mars:

"Thy first asylum and thy first repair
    Shall be the mighty Lombard's courtesy
    Whose arms the eagle on the ladder bear.
Such kindliness shall he accord to thee
    That, 'twixt you two, of answer and request
    That which is ever last, the first shall be.
With him shalt see another, so imprest
    At birth by influence of the planet red,
    His works shall be recorded with the best.
Of him but little hath as yet been said,
    So young is he; for years no more than nine
    These heavenly wheels have circled round his head.
But ere great Hal the Gascon undermine,
    His manly virtue shall begin to show,
    Heedless of toil, heedless of silver coin.
The time shall come when all the world shall know
    His whole magnificence — renown too great
    To suffer silence even from his foe.
Wait thou for him, his largesses await.
    The fates of many mortals he shall weave,
    Beggars and rich exchanging their estate.
This much of him in custody receive,
    But tell it not . . ." and then he spake of things
    Which those who see them scarcely shall believe.
                       Par., XVII, 70–93.

For Italy, for the Empire, for the world, the poet hoped much of Can Grande. For himself, too, he may have looked to a great future under the patronage of the young Vicar General. He may have had a vision of Florence regenerate, subject to the beneficent government of the Scaliger, with himself, as an expert in Florentine affairs, officiating as the ruler's trusted counselor. Thus, with great cogency, argues Professor Fletcher, who, like myself, identifies with Can Grande the Veltro prophesied at the beginning of Dante's *Hell*.

However, it is the admission of wrongdoing that now concerns us. The confessional character of Dante's interview with Beatrice in Eden — the central episode of the poem — is emphasized beyond possibility of error. This colloquy assumes, indeed, the formal proportions of the three stages of the Sacrament of Penance, ending with Absolution. After her recital of his sinfulness, "To such a charge," says Beatrice,

> "To such a charge
> Thine own confession must be mated now."
> > *Purg.*, xxxi, 5–6.

And this confession is at last uttered,

> Gurgling its way with gush of tears and sighs.
> > *Purg.*, xxxi, 20.

> Fear mingled with confusion found the word
> And pusht a "yes" so feeble from my lips
> That ears without the eyes had never heard.
> > *Purg.*, xxxi, 13–15.

Her worshipper, so Beatrice tells the attendant angels, was by nature and by special grace so endowed that he might have borne every good fruit; but the richest soil, if uncultivated, gives the worst growth.

> "Awhile my countenance sustained his soul;
> > As long as he my youthful eyes could see,
> > I led him with me toward the proper goal.
> When life I changed to immortality,
> > Upon the threshold of my second age,
> > He gave him to another, leaving me.

> From fleshly risen up to ghostly stage,
>> In beauty and in virtue more adept,
>> His heart and fancy I did less engage;
> And into paths untrue he turned and stept,
>> Pursuing false appearances of good,
>> Which never any promise fully kept."
>>> *Purg.*, xxx, 124–132.

"Why," asks Beatrice of her repentant lover, "why did you ever stray from me?"

> Weeping, I spake: "The things of now and here
>> With false attraction turned aside my steps
>> As soon as e'er your face did disappear."
>>> *Purg.*, xxxi, 34–36.

That he may be more ashamed of his recreancy, and another time may be stronger when he shall hear the Sirens sing, Beatrice bids him listen to what she is about to say. Her death, she argues, should have proved to him the deceptiveness of mortal charms.

> "When wounded first by disappointment's bow,
>> For fragile things, thou shouldst have taken wing
>> And followed me, who was no longer so.
> No little maid or other passing thing
>> Should e'er have bent thy pinions down to earth,
>> There to await the arrow's second sting."
>>> *Purg.*, xxxi, 55–60.

"Little maid or other passing thing": such is the Siren against which Dante is to be fortified. Whether the "little maid" be allegorical or carnal, this is surely no description of Lady Philosophy.

In any case, the poet's deviation from the cult of his "most gentle" Beatrice was sinful. That we know, because, after drinking of Lethe, which removes the memory of sin, and of sin only, Dante has no recollection of his infidelity.

I answered then: "I have no memory
    That e'er from your allegiance I did stray.
    No recollection of it censures me."
"Now, if the memory has past away,"
    She smiling said, "the cause of it inquire! —
    Of Lethe thou hast drunk this very day.
If smoke be certainly a sign of fire,
    Then thy forgetting is a certain proof
    That sin was in the shift of thy desire."

                 Purg., XXXIII, 91–99.

Confession, however, is not restricted to this scene, where it is so solemn, so impressive, so explicit. We may see it inconspicuously pervading all the poet's journey through the second realm of the dead. For Dante's Purgatory is a place of penance; and while, in the literal sense, his narrative tells of his passing through seven rings of penitents, engaged in cleansing themselves of the seven capital vices, allegorically he is himself undergoing discipline. Wherever, then, he seems to share in the pains of Purgatory, we may infer that the vice punished in the terrace where he suffers is one to which he considered himself addicted, a vice of which he must purge himself ere he attain the purity of heart that shall enable him to see God.

The first and lowest terrace affords discipline for pride, the worst of vices and the basis of all sin. Here the penitents creep stooping, crushed like caryatids under the weight of great blocks of stone which they carry on their backs — an image of agonizing self-humiliation.

'Neath roof or ceiling, to afford a rest,
    Sometimes doth human shape as corbel serve,
    And seems to press its knees against its chest
(Which sight the kind beholder may unnerve
    With real anguish for unreal pain):
    E'en so were these, when I did close observe —

Contracted, though, with less or greater strain
   According to the more or less they bore;
   And e'en the patientest, it seemed, would fain
Cry out with tears: "I can endure no more!"
                         Purg., x, 130–139.

Now, Dante, as he walks and talks with these, assumes their posture — ostensibly, the better to see and listen, but in the "allegorical and true sense," to take part in their penance. As he hears the story of Omberto Aldobrandesco, count of Santafiore, an example of the pride of birth, he begins to stoop.

I downward bent my face, better to list;
   When one, not he who spake, it did befall,
   Beneath his hampering burden gave a twist,
And saw and knew me and let out a call,
   Keeping his eyes with difficulty fixt
   On me, who walkt low crouching with them all.
                         Purg., xi, 73–78.

This second spirit is Oderisi of Gubbio, a famous illuminator in his day. He exemplifies the pride of art. The pride of birth and the artist's pride Dante knew right well; of both he gives evidence, even in Heaven. One thinks at once of the majestic introduction to the second canto of the *Paradise*, and of the already cited expression of hope of the laurel crown, as instances of glory in the poet's craft; one may add the rating of himself with the great poets of antiquity in the fourth canto of *Hell*. As an avowal of family pride, one turns to the beginning of *Paradise*, canto XXI, where Dante apologizes for his self-satisfaction in the presence of his noble ancestor, Cacciaguida.

With Oderisi, then, the poet crawls along, harkening while his companion homilizes on the vanity of human fame (incidentally hinting at the immortality in store for

Dante) and while he tells the story of a third soul, Pro-
venzano Salvani, who is doing penance for the pride of
power.

> At even pace, like oxen yoked in twain,
>   With that encumbered spirit I did creep
>   While Virgil's kindness let me thus remain.
> But when he said: "Pass by him, rise and leap!
>   For here 'tis good for each, with sail and oar,
>   To drive his boat its swiftest o'er the deep," —
> My body its uprightness did restore,
>   Erect, as man should walk, altho my thoughts
>   Were left subdued and prostrate, humbled sore.
>   *Purg.*, XII, 1–9.

Next to pride is envy. Seated on the ground, along the
wall, like beggars, are the envious — blinded, their eyes
being sewed up with wire. This is a sin with which Dante
feels himself but slightly tainted; so he tells one of the
penitents, a certain Sapia of Siena.

> "Mine eyes I yet shall forfeit even thus,
>   But not for long; for little is the sin
>   Committed by their glances envious.
> Far greater is the fear my soul is in
>   Of that impending punishment below,
>   Whose weight already seems my limbs to pin."
>   *Purg.*, XIII, 133–138.

Anger is a fault not incompatible with our conception
of the great Florentine; and the cure for anger — a thick,
black smoke which signifies the stifling of irascibility —
chokes Dante as it chokes the other penitents. We are on
the third terrace of Purgatory, having traversed the rings
of pride and envy.

> Thro' eventide we walked, and lookt ahead
>   As far along as human eyes could flit
>   To meet the setting sunbeams, bright and red,

When lo! a smoke came rolling bit by bit
   Along the pathway toward us, dark as night.
   No space was there to turn aside from it.
Clean air it took from us, and power of sight.

  .   .   .   .

Darkness of Hell, darkness of night bereft
   Of every star, beneath a scanty sky,
   So black with clouds that nothing light is left,
Did ne'er with veil so heavy shroud mine eye —
   Nor one whose harshness so the senses tried,
   As did the smoke which we were covered by.
For smart, the eye could open not abide;
   Whereat my trusty guide, with ready skill,
   His shoulder offered, drawing up beside.
As blind man close pursues his leader's will,
   Lest he be lost, and lest he bump his head
   On something that may hurt, or haply kill,
Thus I thro' dirty, bitter air was led,
   And listened anxious to my master's voice.
   "Be not lopt off from me," was all he said.
                   Purg., xv, 139–xvi, 15.

With sinful irascibility we must not confound righteous indignation, the feeling which the sight of sin should properly arouse in the godly. The distinction is made very clear in the part of *Hell* which deals with wrath. Here, amidst the mad mangling of the angry in the Stygian mire, stands forth conspicuous Dante's attitude of abhorrence, excited by the onset of that arrogant Florentine bully, Filippo Argenti. And this moral posture meets with the rapturous approval of reason, embodied in Virgil.

Both Virgil's arms unto my neck did cleave;
   He kist my face. "Indignant soul!" he cried,
   "Blessed the woman who did thee conceive!
This person in the world was puft with pride.
   No bit of goodness decorates his name;
   And therfore fury doth his spirit ride.

How many plume themselves on kingly fame
    Who here shall dwell like pigs in nastiness
    And leave behind them despicable blame!"

Next of the seven capital vices is sloth, or spiritual sluggishness, due to inadequate love of God. To be told that Dante was slothful would put our credulity to a test all too severe; and happily we are spared that strain. For in the incessant running which constitutes the ghostly exercise of the ring of sloth our poet takes no part.

A trial awaits us, however, on the terrace of avarice and prodigality — these two opposite sins being punished together in Purgatory, as in Hell. Now, we have here but the faintest of indications of any bite of conscience on Dante's part; yet the one little signal is worth attention. As he passes among the prostrate forms of misers and prodigals, he is pricked with sympathy, even while recognizing the fitness of the penalty:

    E condoleami alla giusta vendetta.
    And righteous retribution gave me pain.
                    Purg., xxi, 6.

Can his sympathy have been bestowed on the hoarders? Listen to the terms in which the poet apostrophizes the ravening wolf — immoderate love of money:

    A curse upon thee, wolf of hoary age,
        That more than other animals hast prey,
        For never sated is thy ravening rage!
    O heaven, whose circling earthly things obey
        (As we on earth apparently believe),
        When cometh One to drive this beast away?
                   Purg., xx, 10–15.

Can Dante have been a miser? Certainly not: few things did he hate as he hated avarice. But may he not have thought himself something of a spendthrift? Likely

enough; else why should he have twice taken such pains
to point the doctrine that prodigality, though not in general thought of as a sin, is really just as wicked as hoard-
ing? The spender is popular, his neighbors call him a good
fellow — especially the literary men, nearly all parasites
in Dante's day, who sang the praises of the vice which
nourished them; whereas, in point of fact, he is guilty of
the same lack of restraint that characterizes the miser,
whom nobody loves. From the vigor with which the author forces this unwelcome truth upon us, we may infer
that it had forced itself, all unwelcome, upon him. Into
the rôle of Statius, Dante's representative prodigal, our
poet seems to infuse much of his own sentiment and some
of his own experience.

With gluttony, sixth of the vices, Dante shows no
sympathy, although he does manifest pity and affection
for his former friend, Forese Donati, a victim to that
habit; and likewise he expresses compassion, in Hell, for
the lost gourmand, Ciacco. Gluttony, like avarice, like
sloth, is alien to our poet, whom we have found slightly
infected with envy, over prone to wrath, dangerously
proud, and, as we have had some reason to conjecture,
addicted to excessive expenditure.

Too loose in spending, he was also (in his own judgment) too loose in loving. And this voluptuous habit is
the hardest to correct. Even the will to reform is lacking;
the voice of reason speaks in vain; only the thought of
Beatrice has power to turn him to his fiery discipline. In
the other penances of Purgatory, the traveler willingly
shares, whenever they are needful to him; but at the
burning cure for amorousness he balks, until brought to
his senses by the hope of becoming worthy of his lost love.
This struggle is the theme of the most dramatic scene in

the *Purgatorio*. Before the wall of fire, on the seventh
terrace, the wayfarers have come — Dante and his kind
companions, Virgil and Statius. Just outside the blaze,
on the edge of the shelf, stands an angel, and sings.

Singing, on flameless brink the angel stood,
    And "Blessed are the pure in heart" it cried
    More vitally than mortal voices could.
"Dear souls, your further progress is denied
    Until the fire shall bite. Now enter here,
    And watch for singing on the other side."
These were its words when we had drawn anear.
    As one who lowered in the grave hath been,
    E'en such was I, on hearing it, for fear.
Clasping my hands, I over them did lean,
    And stared into the fire, remembering burned
    Bodies of men which once mine eyes had seen.
My loving escorts both upon me turned.
    "My son, my son!" Virgil began to cry:
    "Here torture, yes; not death! Hast thou not learned?
Remember, O remember! Think, if I
    On Geryon's back thy flesh did safely bear,
    Shall I be wanting now that God is nigh?
Believe for certain, shouldst thou linger there
    A thousand years within the hollow flame,
    It could not strip thee of a single hair.
On thy belief I make too strong a claim?
    Step near it, try the fringes of thy dress
    With thine own hands, and put thy fright to shame.
Cast off, O! do cast off all timorousness!
    Turn hither, son, come gallantly and free!"
    Yet obstinate I stood and conscienceless.
When he beheld me standing stubbornly,
    Angered a little, "Mind, my son," he said,
    "This fire's a wall 'twixt Beatrice and thee."
As Pyramus upturned his dying head
    At Thisbe's name, and looked at her, they say,
    What time the mulberry was colored red;

Thus, all my hardness softening away,
    I faced my leader, when the name I heard
    Which blooms afresh within me every day.
Whereat he shook his head and spake this word:
    "Well! shall we dally here?" And smiled again,
    As at a child who by a fruit is stirred;
Then led the way within the fiery pain,
    Requesting Statius after me to pass,
    Who many a mile had walked between us twain.
So measureless the baking heat, alas!
    When I was in it, that for coolness' sake
    I would have thrown me into boiling glass.
My gentle father said, to ease my ache:
    "Her eyes already do I seem to see";
    And constantly of Beatrice he spake.

Purg., xxvii, 7–54.

Having gathered Dante's confession, bit by bit, from his *Purgatory*, let us see whether aught may be gleaned from his *Hell*; for the whole *Comedy*, I believe, was written in a frankly confessional mood. In the first part of the poem the punishments are symbols, not of penances, but of sins. What we must watch is the poet's attitude toward each one. His own reaction is not always identical with that of Virgil, or Reason. For instance, while the disciple is moved to tears by the evil plight of magicians and fortune-tellers, the master feels only indignation, and utters a sharp rebuke. "How could I help weeping?" Dante asks, remembering the cruel distortion of humanity that he viewed, looking down into the sorcerers' ditch from a natural bridge.

Upon the rugged bridge, surely I wept,
    Leaning against a crag. But Virgil said:
    "Hast still the foolishness of mortals kept?
Now pity lives, which rightly should be dead.
    For who is more accursed than the man
    Who from divine decree averts his head?"

Inf., xx, 25–30.

At the spectacle of hypocrisy, Virgil is filled with wonder. By blasphemy he is violently shocked. His intolerance of sorcery may have been contrived by the poet, as d'Ovidio has brilliantly suggested, to vindicate him from medieval report which made Virgil himself a sorcerer. Another purpose may have been an avowal, on Dante's part, that his own inclination to sympathize with such misuse of great intelligence was contrary to reason.

For Dante, throughout his *Hell*, does manifest fellow-feeling with those who erred from the pride of mental superiority. It must be remembered that the poet, in this part of his journey, is still in a state of sin. Toward the heretic he is respectful, and toward the eloquent and venturesome; for the great-minded suicide he feels respect and pity. When the offender is one who has deserved well of his country, Dante's feeling is sanctioned by his master.

Mean fraud, on the other hand, excites the poet's scorn. He has no softness for alchemists, counterfeiters, grafters, liars. With the simonist, his contempt expresses itself in mockery. Thieves are horrible. But above all he loathes flatterers. Misers and usurers fare little better. Disgust is aroused by gluttony, cold hatred by ingratitude and treachery, vindictiveness by brutal arrogance; and this last sentiment, as we have seen in the episode of Filippo Argenti, is warmly approved by Reason.

It appears that such indications of Dante's character tally well enough with those afforded by the *Purgatory*, as far as these latter go. In like harmony is his intense sympathy with the amorous; he swoons with pity on hearing the story of Francesca. Another weakness, his tendency to indulge in strife, is perhaps borne out by the unhealthy pleasure he takes in listening to altercation — to the vul-

gar quarrel between master Adam, the counterfeiter, and
Sinon of Troy, the liar, in the tenth pouch of the eighth
circle.

> In list'ning to them, all absorbed was I,
>> Until my master warned me. "Now look out!
>> To pick a bone with thee I'm mighty nigh."
> Hearing myself rebuked with angry shout,
>> I turned to him, impelled by such a shame
>> That in my memory still it spins about.
> And like a man who dreams he suffers blame
>> And, dreaming, wishes it were only dream,
>> Craving what is, as 't were not, just the same,
> So I, who speechless my repentance deem,
>> Long to excuse myself and all the while
>> I do excuse me, silent tho' I seem.
> "Less shame can wash away a fault more vile
>> Than thine hath been," the kindly master cried.
> "Unburden thee of bitterness and bile!
> And see that I be ever at thy side
>> If fate again thy presence shall require
>> Where folk in like dispute be occupied.
> Desire to hear such talk is low desire."
>> *Inf.*, xxx, 130–148.

Of like nature is the fascination exercised on him by the
sight of the mangled forms of the schismatics and trouble-
makers, horribly and strangely mutilated, like the bodies
piled on some impossible battle-field.

> The multitude, the mutilations weird
>> Had so befuddled mine enhungered eyes
>> That they to pause and weep were not afeard.
> "Why dost thou stare and stare?" my Virgil cries.
>> "How comes it, all thine interest down below
>> Amidst the sorry mangled shadows lies?
> Thou hast not done in other places so."
>> *Inf.*, xxix, 1–7.

Beside the moral faults thus directly or indirectly
avowed, there is appropriate place for the confession of

an intellectual vice, the tendency to take too short a cut
to conclusions. This is an offense against reason, and
Virgil snubs the offender for it in the passage with which
I opened this discussion. More explicitly he chides him
later on, while the poets, in the dusk of Hell, are approaching the brink of the central pit. There, ranged
round the edge, is a circle of towering shapes — im-
prisoned giants, one of whom is Nimrod with his hunter's
horn.

> Here, less it was than night and less than day,
>   And so the bow of sight but feebly shot;
>   When lo! a horn was blowing far away
> So loud, a thunder-clap had sounded not;
>   Which made my eyes along its course to go,
>   Contrariwise, toward a certain spot.
> After the dire defeat, where, doomed to woe,
>   Great Charles's holy peers their life-blood shed,
>   So terribly did Roland never blow.
> But little after I had turned my head,
>   Towers high and many I did seem to spy.
>   "What is this city, master, pray," I said.
> "Too fast and far afield thy sight doth fly —
>   Too far, in darkness; and the consequence
>   Must needs be this: thou seest things awry.
> How badly distance can deceive the sense,
>   On thine arrival thou shalt understand.
>   So spur thyself more speedily from thence."
> Then tenderly he took me by the hand,
>   And added: "Ere we penetrate so far,
>   Lest thou be sore bewildered on the rand,
> I tell thee, they not towers but giants are."
>   *Inf.*, XXXI, 10–31.

The normal, orderly course of perception is illustrated,
in the Garden of Eden, by Dante's gradual cognizance of
the seven golden candlesticks which march at the head of
the pageant of the Church. We are in a vernal wood, and
a sweet melody is coursing through the luminous air.

And while I walked, entranced with everything,
  Foretasting Heaven, eternal joys among,
  And still for greater gladness hungering,
In front of us, gleaming its way along,
  The air grew firelike 'neath each verdant bough;
  And then the melody was heard as song.
If e'er for you, O Virgins of my vow,
  Hunger or cold or sleeplessness I bore,
  My need commands I ask my guerdon now.
Let Helicon for me its waters pour
  And let Urania's choir my trial ease,
  Thought-passing things in verse to carry o'er.
A little farther on, seven golden trees
  The distance made deceptively appear,
  Which intervened between ourselves and these.
But when at last I had approached so near
  That, stead of treacherous generality,
  Each proper trait was made by closeness clear,
The power which makes us rationally see
  Perceived as candlesticks the golden light
  And marked "Hosannah" in the harmony.
The fair array above was shining bright,
  Clearer by far than moon in cloudless sky
  In middle month in middle of the night.
I turned about with wonder-stricken eye
  To kindly Virgil; but his startled look
  With e'en as great amazement made reply.
                              Purg., xxix, 31–56.

The critical part of the above citation reads in the text
thus, and may be partially elucidated by comparison with
two passages on the *Banquet* (III, ix, and IV, viii):

Ma quand' i' fui sì presso di lor fatto
  Che l'obbietto comun, che'l senso inganna,
  Non perdea per distanza alcun suo atto,
La virtù ch' a ragion discorso ammanna,
  Sì com' elli eran candelabri apprese,
  E ne le voci del cantare, "*Osanna*."

Which may be literally rendered, line by line:

But when I had come so close to them
  That the variously perceptible, which deceives the
    sense,
  Lost none of its attributes by remoteness,
That power which provides reason with discrimination,
  Apprehended that they were candlesticks,
  And apprehended "Hosannah" in the voices of the
    song.

The danger of over-hasty inferences, and self-satisfied
retention of them, is set forth in Heaven by St. Thomas
Aquinas, commenting on Dante's faulty interpretation
of the phrase "no second ever rose," *non surse il s'econdo,*
which has to do with Solomon and need not concern us
here. What interests us now is the general admonition:

"Let this example make thy motion slow,
  Like weary men's, with lead upon their feet,
  Toward a 'yes' unseen or hidden 'no.'
He who doth promptly 'yes' or 'no' repeat,
  Without defining what is in his mind,
  Among the stupid hath a lowly seat;
For reason oft to error is inclined
  By premise immature that wins it o'er,
  And then doth self-esteem the judgment bind.
Vainly and worse than vainly quits the shore
  Who fishes for the truth without the skill,
  Returning homeward poorer than before.
Abundant witnesses your history fill:
  Melissus, Bryson, and Parmenides,
  Who, knowing not their goal, kept walking still.
Thus did Sabellius, Arius, all the race
  Of fools who mis-reflected Holy Writ,
  As crooked glass distorts a comely face.
Let people hold their judgment back a bit
  And be not rash as he who counts his corn
  Before the summertide hath ripened it.

For I have seen on every winter morn
 A briar stiff and wild, until the spring,
 When lo! upon its crest a rose was born;
Yea, once beheld, as straight as any string,
 A vessel speeding over all its way
 E'en to the port, and sink while entering.
Ah! let not Tom or Dick or Harry say,
 When this one steals and that one goes to church,
 He knows their sentence on the Judgment Day;
For one may climb, the other, downward lurch.
                    Par., XIII, 112–142.

Knowledge, like logic, is progressive. Step by step we must move on, from one partial truth to another, until at last the final truth be reached. Then, and then only, the mind shall be at peace. Such is Dante's reflection, when, in Paradise, he has listened to Beatrice's elucidation of the problem of the will — the distinction between the will absolute and the will conditioned. This important difference once grasped, the disciple proceeds to generalize from present and past experiences, justifying doubt and explaining its function in rational procedure:

I clearly see, our mind has no repose
 Unless that Truth illuminate its quest
 Outside of which no truth whatever grows.
Therein it sleeps, like beastie in its nest,
 As soon as found; and we can find it out,
 Else never could our aspirations rest.
Now that is why, in likeness of a sprout,
 Ever there springeth up at foot of truth —
 Chasing us topward, hill by hill — a doubt.
                    Par., IV, 124–132.

Infinity

WEATHER, like man, is a thing of habit. On whichever road it gets started, a wet one or a dry one, change is difficult. A long stretch of sunny days will be followed, almost certainly, by more sunshine; while every day of persistent rain makes any subsequent clearing more unlikely. As to the deficiency in precipitation, that is chronic; it is like a rusty weathervane, which, all unmoved, lets the wind blow where it listeth. The deluges of last July affected it not; neither will the drought which doubtless is to follow in September. When old Noah emerged from the Ark and purchased his first newspaper after the Flood, what heading at once caught his eye? "Rainfall still three inches below normal." In matters pluvial, normalcy is a goal always to be sought and never attained.

If my faith in official reports is inadequate, still weaker is my confidence in wise old saws. "Rain before seven, clear before eleven" owes all its impressiveness to the chance of rime. Supposing seven had rimed with twelve, would the weather have been different? Or with eight? Rimes were deceivers ever; Plato was playing safe in his exclusion of poets from the Republic. "Thirty days hath September." Think what would have happened if the Julian calendar had been constructed on a different rime-scheme! Poe's Raven might have had to come a-tapping in the chill July.

But whether in rime or in free verse, our traditional

prognostications have nothing at all to do with meteoro-
logical lore; they hark back to superstitions of the paleo-
zoic age. "When the days begin to lengthen, then the
cold begins to strengthen" is an echo of the primeval conflict between the Demon of Darkness and the Sun-God.
A horse totem is still present in the dictum that "mares'
tails mean rain." When anyone says to me, "Stars above
and none below, sartain sign o' rain or snow" or "Thun-
der in the morning, sailors take warning," I want to tell
him to go to the Golden Bow-Wows. He is merely re-
hearsing the incantations of a forgotten mythology.

Not that myths are to be despised. Without doubt,
mythologies, which are the religions of the past, were
once matters of implicit and universal belief; just as religions, which so many people would now define as the
mythologies of the present, were at their beginning stark
reality to all. Why are they no longer so? The difficulty,
I take it, lies in the idea of infinity. The universe has
grown too big. There are too many sparrows for any
Watcher to watch, too many hairs for any Counter to
count. But if the Beyond does not really give personal
attention to all these minutiæ, it is useless to pray and
it makes no difference whether a Beyond exists or not.
Thus men are driven either to blank materialism or to
a poetic but unsatisfactory pantheism. All for lack of
a concept of infinity. For it is obvious that an infinite
Guardian could watch over the trillion needs of a billion
people as closely and as easily as an earthly mother can
watch over her brood of three.

For a man of any enlightened epoch actually and in-
telligently to make religion his own — to harbor faith in a
Mind that directs throughout eternity every detail of the
universe — he must form a notion of the infinite. We

glibly use the word, as our forefathers did; but whereas to them it meant something imaginable though intangible, to us it conveys nothing at all. Our finite has come to be so overwhelming that aught surpassing it is simply meaningless. Infinity is something that lies beyond the scope of number or any other measure. When the numbers known to men were small, infinity lay near; now that the figures familiar to our astronomers, our physicists, our geologists, even to our financiers, are infinitely in excess of our fathers' infinity, how are we to think of an infinity infinitely more infinite still? What does a distance of "a million light-years" signify to us? And how are we to conceive of anything incalculably longer — so much longer that it has no length? And a thing inexpressibly smaller — so small that it has no smallness. For length and smallness imply comparison. Insecurely poised between the infinitely great and the infinitely little: such is man, according to Pascal. "Entre ces deux abîmes de l'infini et du néant, il tremblera dans la vue de ces merveilles."

When Daniel declared, "Thousand thousands ministered unto him, and ten thousand times ten thousand stood before him," he was voicing infinity; yet to us these are tiny figures. In a medieval description of hell, the question is raised: "How many are the punishments?" And the answer comes: "The punishments are 54,000; and if there were a hundred men speaking from the beginning of the world until now, and every one had five hundred iron tongues, they could not name all the punishments of hell." Here is a number so impossibly great that it ceases to be a number and becomes a symbol of infinity. How closely, in those days, the infinite encircled us! A "million" was at first only a vague "big thousand." When the stars were but some hundreds of thousands of miles away and the sun was the *ne plus ultra* of bigness among them, when atoms (assuming that they existed) were indivisible and represented the extreme of littleness, when the whole age of the world from Creation to Judgment was only eight thousand years or so, it was not impossible for a potent imagination to conjure up the thought of an all-encompassing Intelligence that was responsible for all and had cognizance of all. Now it has got beyond us. But can we not catch up? Are we permanently incapacitated? Has our wealth blinded us forever? We have not been trying very long. The preposterous figures with which we now have to deal are of very recent date indeed; our minds are not yet adjusted to them. We are new-rich in numbers, and, like all *nouveaux riches*, we require time — perhaps several generations — before we can recover from the giddiness of transcendent ciphering and settle back into quiet respectability. I have read in some nature-book that crows can count up to three, but no further. Some savages, I believe, limit their arithmetic to ten, everything higher being only a vague bigness, like the medieval infinity, or else "more tens," like our light-years. Now we accept a million as a matter of course, although I greatly doubt whether any of my readers has ever seen a million or ever counted so high.

In an old number of *Fliegende Blätter* a party of sightseers is visiting an observatory. The astronomer, who has been discoursing of stellar distances, interrupts his lecture to observe: "I am talking of millions; but I suppose not one of you can form any conception of a million." "Excuse me," retorts one of the company, bullet-headed, self-complacent, a huge watch-chain stretching across his plutocratic paunch, "I own three." Well, if he does own them, he cannot count them. Never can he

taste the delight that gladdened the old-fashioned miser
(for instance, the white-headed miscreant in the *Cloches
de Corneville*) — the delight, I mean, of counting his gold.
Really, what is the use of being a miser nowadays?

Perhaps there are no misers left. Indeed, everybody,
rich or poor, seems bent on spending all he can get, or
more, as fast as he can get it, or faster. The luxuries of one
generation (as J.-J. Rousseau told us long ago) become
the necessities of the next. Our conception of wealth
has changed as rapidly, and almost as bewilderingly, as
our notion of number. One Sunday, not long ago, at
the risk of my life, I traversed a suburban district on
a bicycle. Side-streets were choked with cars parked,
parking, and deparking, while every avenue was one immense, continuous torrent, a flood-maddened Mississippi,
of automobiles. Habit impelled me bitterly to make inner
comment on "the idle rich." Then I began to scan the
occupants. Workingmen, mostly in their working clothes,
wives just escaped from the kitchen, numberless children
tightly packed: that is what they were, nearly all of them.
And I began to doubt whether the Ford were an unmiti-
gated evil.

Again, on another Sunday, I rode through the Middle-
sex Fells Reservation. That picturesque wood was alive
with little picnic parties. Hundreds of families, having
arrived in their cars and parked the same by the wayside,
were spending the day in old-time sylvan diversions,
enjoying the spring, enjoying one another's company,
enjoying also the luncheon they had brought with them.
Once more I had to reconsider my habitual estimate of
the automobile; I will not say, of the flivver, because,
while all these people were of the poorer class, many of the
machines were anything but poor.

Another prejudice, too, I came near revising — my
aversion from Prohibition. Theoretically the Eighteenth
Amendment was as unjustifiable as ever; but it really
seemed to have brought prosperity and gayety to no end
of people. For there could be no doubt concerning the
contrast between the present holiday conduct of these
same trippers and the Sunday conditions of their like,
twenty years before. The latter were familiar enough to
us all. We hated them, they sickened us; but we thought
them normal and inevitable. The father of the house
would be in a dead stupor, sleeping off a drunk, with little
prospect of fitness for work on Monday morning. The
mother, perhaps marked with signs of recent altercation,
would be sullenly drudging away at the housework. The
daughters, in pairs, one could see strolling through the
streets, with vacant shrill laughter trying to attract the
attention of young men. The boys would be lounging
on corners, spitting copious tobacco-juice and loudly
exchanging remarks so stomach-turning that the least
squeamish would gladly go six blocks out of his way
rather than pass by them, were it not that every other
corner was equally nasty. Such was the Sunday of our
working classes before the advent of the Volstead Act and
the auto. Can it be that "somehow Good shall come of
Water and of Mud"? Is it possible that a wrong shall set
so many creatures aright? No, it is inadmissible that
good should flow out of evil. To be sure, there was the
Panama Canal. . . . The question is pretty big for a finite
intelligence. Possibly there is something amiss with our
definitions of good and bad. Our conception of our rights
may change, with our estimate of our own importance, as
varies our idea of number and of infinity.

Many of our criteria of germaneness have been altered,

some of them very rapidly. Supposing you had to recommend a young man for a position: would you do it in the same terms that you employed forty years ago? In those days the most important requisite was that the candidate be "a Christian gentleman" — and the phrase did not then mean simply "not a Jew." Not so long ago, a northern college needed an instructor in the Classics. From an old-fashioned Southern community came a nomination: "In the first place, Mr. Bloodgood is a Christian gentleman, a Baptist, and a regular church-goer. He is a son of Colonel Bloodgood, well known in this State, a nephew of the illustrious General Bloodgood, a grandson of Judge Bloodgood of Bloodgood. His mother was a Stirling, daughter of Colonel Robert Stirling of Stirling. We commend him without reservation." From the cold-blooded Northern president came the reply: "We are in search of a man to teach Greek and Latin. We are not looking for a man for breeding purposes."

In a state of flux are our values, our numbers, our infinity. The weather alone is constant.

Ivanhoe Street

SOME cities have an East Side, generally tough, and a more genteel West Side. Why the points of the compass should thus affect the character of the inhabitants, I have never been able to discover; but East will be East, and West will be West. Even Boston, whose social distinctions were originally rather latitudinal than longitudinal, developed, long since, a peculiarly Brahminic West End, which subsequently, nourished by countless tipcarts and piledrivers, grew into the Back Bay. At the opposite pole from the Back Bay, socially and topographically, was the South Cove, which really lay east; thus, for all her desire to be different, the Hub City did come to tolerate, though without due recognition, a longitudinal stratification. At present, as all men know, we have but the Back Bay and the Non Back Bay — the Occident on the one hand, and on the other a coalition of Orient with the realms of Boreas and Auster, united in the resolve to exclude exclusive Hesperia from participation in public affairs.

Half a century ago, although the name West End had already appeared in Bostonian geography, the great division was between North End and South End, the former (as a residential quarter) tough and poor, the latter respectable and well-to-do. Aloof from both stood Beacon Hill. The Mason and Dixie line, as I remember it, was uncertain, generally shifting to the southward. The North End, indeed, being the elder branch of the city, still retained some good old streets and good old houses and good old families, erect amid the tide of squalor that was rising around them. The South End, too, had its shabby sections, despite the prevalence of prosperity; its architecture, uniformly of brick, betrayed two definite strata, a paleolithic type of solidly built, short, squat, flat-bosomed dwellings in the more downtown part, while farther uptown flourished the neolithic swell front, high, proud, with a little front yard, a tall flight of stone steps, and a basement entrance underneath. The small underlying porch seemed especially designed for children to play house; and the slanting stone balustrades beside the front steps furnished perfect slides, when a mistaken esthetic aspiration had not cut them up into ornamental designs. One of the neolithic triumphs was Blackstone Square, coldly majestic with its iron-fenced park, a fountain playing in the middle. Matching it across Washington Street was Franklin Square, built on the same plan, but a shade less magnificent.

From residence to boarding-house, from boarding-house to shop or institution, such has been the general evolution of these stately quarters. The first innovation in Franklin Square, however, contained no open threat of a decline; for on its south side sprang up the St. James Hotel, whose splendid proportions encroached upon the old graveyard in the rear. My earliest visual impression of death came from the inspection of bones and skulls turned up to make room for the foundations of the haughty hostelry, the dead giving way to the unborn. Death itself is but transient, whatever the Ecclesiast may say.

Vieil amant du soleil, qui gémissais ainsi,
L'irrévocable mort est un mensonge aussi.

In its proudest day the St. James entertained President Grant; I can still see my father lifting me above the crowd to watch the great general — my first idol — come down the stairs. A victim to the centripetal movement that has ruled Boston business, the hotel first yielded its spaciousness to the New England Conservatory of Music, and later became the Franklin Square House, a home for working-girls.

One building hard by I cannot look upon without a pang, and yet some fascination draws me to it year by year. On Brookline Street, once a modest but self-respecting swell-front home, now a tenement-house sordidly unashamed. Like Boston itself, the structure has developed by accretion before and behind. The little front area, with its locust tree, whose graceful branches used to wave against the windows of the second story, has been pushed out of existence by a vulgar excrescent shop. In the rear, a long, unwholesome extension fills up most of the back yard that was once so full of associations: the plants which in city soil and city shadow obstinately resisted all efforts to make them live; the creeper which finally did creep, up and up the back fence, lovingly measured day by day, until (ecstatic moment!) it sent a shoot over the top — only to be plucked by the careless hand of a chance passer-by. Of that ruthless destroyer I never saw more than the clutching hand as it appeared over the fence, and the vanishing back as I rushed to the gate to see what manner of demon could do such a deed. But I hated him (and, I fear, still hate him) as I never hated any other man, save one. Let that one now be held up to the obloquy he deserves! A mouse had been caught in a trap; by long and tearful pleading I had obtained its pardon; the trap was taken to the back gate and the prisoner released in the back alley. "Vain is the help of man." A stroller, espying the tiny fugitive, sprang forward, and, with one stamp of his great foot, crushed out of it all life and all semblance of mousehood. That was the one moment of my existence when I wanted to believe in Hell.

Looking up at the back of the house I can still, I think, detect the window of the little room where I had scarlet fever and diphtheria, and enjoyed the distinction — never equaled since — of being about to die. It is odd that my earliest clear recollection of life should be the consciousness of parting from it. What influence, if any, that precocious renunciation had on my philosophy, I cannot say. At any rate, I can relieve your anxiety at once by assuring you that, like Tiny Tim, I did *not* die. But my narrow escape gave me a considerable prestige among my playfellows, when I issued forth into the world. I can still recall the pride of my first walk along Sharon Street, escorted by a troop of timidly admiring mates, the most devoted of whom I comforted with a solemn promise that I would not "give it" to them, while the more lukewarm were left, by ambiguous words, in secret dread of extermination.

Sharon Street! Even now I thrill at the sound or the sight of it: my oasis of fellowship in a desert of loneliness. For I must have been abominably lonesome most of the time; an only child, rather sickly, early inclined to introspection, and desperately shy. Sharon Street came to be my haven. It was a small street, with two neat lines of low brick houses — a pioneer street, pushed out into the wilderness beyond Harrison Avenue. There lived a little colony of big musicians, whose children were my refuge. There were the Millers, who made the famous pianos.

There was a favorite cornet-player named Arbuckle; in his house was a boy I did not like very well, because, being much taller than I, he used to twist my arms for fun. I never knew how much fun it is, until, years later, I was old enough to practise the art on boys smaller than I. The most renowned of the musicians was the great bandmaster, Patrick Gilmore, leader of the wonderful Peace Jubilee, which first put the Back Bay on the map and provided, on that new-born territory, a home for the annual visits of the circus. He lived in the first house, and had a dainty little daughter.

One memorable afternoon the Miller boys gave a play in their woodshed. Admission, I think, was two cents. The piece was called "The Mischievous Monkey." Its interest was not primarily psychological, nor was it particularly brilliant in dialogue. Action was its main, perhaps its only, excellence. No! I should say action and costuming, like a musical comedy. It consisted of a series of tricks performed on the other members of the Miller family by the eldest Miller boy, accoutred in a complete and never-to-be-forgotten monkey costume, certainly the work of very skilful grown-up hands.

This, however, was not my earliest theatrical experience. Huge as was my enjoyment of it, I can recall a little by-taste of sophistication, due to a previous attendance at "Blue Beard" in the old Theatre Comique, with my father. Both my father and my mother used to take me to the playhouse, as soon as I was big enough to sit in a chair. Oftenest we did not all three go together; for my mother was more inclined to pieces such as "Fanchon," "East Lynne," "Led Astray," and "Lady Audley's Secret," while my father, a disciple of Carlo Gozzi, rather preferred "Blue Beard," "The Seven Dwarfs,"

"Enchantment," and "The Black Crook." I saw them all.

One more Sharon Street incident haunts my mind. Let me try to get the right atmosphere, for atmosphere is all there is to it. Dusk. You know how curiously it affects people, what a feeling of nervous exhilaration it gives. With children, you must remember (having undoubtedly been a child yourself), this deliciously uncanny sensation is intensified, I think in proportion to their youth. And the less frequent the experience, the higher the tension. One autumn day we—four of us, little tots of five or so — were allowed to walk up and down Sharon Street at dusk. After some minutes of deep-breathing silence, amid the darkening shadows, one of the party remarked, in the matter-of-fact tone of one who knows all about it: "This is the kind of evening when the witches are out." That was the opening of the magic casement. Never since have I felt, nevermore shall I feel, such a sense of supernatural alertness, such sweetness of apprehension, such a consciousness of leading a real life in an unreal world, as we had with us, we four little tots of five or so, now drawn close together, while, on the watch for everything ghostly, we trod the pavement of a faerie Sharon Street.

Commonplace in comparison was the thrill that dwelt in walking around the fountain in Franklin Square on the rim of the great basin. The stone surface being convex, the encircling movement had its excitement when the basin was full of water, as it generally was in those days. A keen excitement, to be sure, but purely realistic, and a bit over-familiar. Of higher interest were the remoter attractions of Union Park and Worcester Square, mysteriously secluded in their foliage, and of palatial Chester Square, with its basin full of goldfishes.

Chester Square was close to the Neck. Boston Neck was once a real neck, a very swanlike one, such as early Victorian ladies wore; and it connected the mainland with the peninsula of Boston — a narrow causeway, just sufficient for the transfer of a line of troops. In my early boyhood its neckishness was still fairly apparent, for the waters of the Back Bay, at high tide, almost reached Tremont Street. I can recall the picture of a diminutive specimen of humanity, just behind Chickering's Piano Factory, planting an onion on the beach, in the expectation that some day it would grow into a broad-spreading onion tree. Now the spot is as hopelessly inland as Ravenna or Aigues-Mortes, not from natural slow upheaval but from rapid artificial dump. The people who started Boston picked a place too small for the greatness that was to ensue; they were already afflicted with the Boston inferiority-complex. In consequence of their absurd underrating of their handiwork, Boston has had to be patched out all around. The vast flats of the Back Bay ultimately have had to renounce their allegiance to Neptune. Long before, the eastern waters, which once penetrated as far as the present Custom House, had been pushed back; and the great North Cove, which extended down into Haymarket Square, had been filled up with earth scooped from the three-pronged summit of Tremont, or Beacon Hill.

Yet this was not enough. Outlying regions had to be drawn in: Noddle's Island, or East Boston; Charlestown, once so smiling between its rivers, now so dingy; the highlands of Roxbury, with their woods and their fantastic masses of puddingstone. The old town of Roxbury, indeed, once extended north almost to the Public Garden, being greater than Boston itself. As to South Boston, its peninsula was early a residential suburb, as may still be guessed from its broad avenues lined with trees. On the ancient mansions that even now retain something of their pride, the doorplates show Irish names; while the rest of the district is crowded with recent incomers from eastern Europe and Asia, incongruously surrounding an elegant marble tower centrally planted on the green of Dorchester Heights — a monument to that battery which drove the British fleet from Boston Harbor.

Dorchester, when I was born there, was a country town. The beautiful view of the sea from the Upper Road still remains; but where are the infinite expanses of goldenrod, where the fields studded with fruitful nut trees? All covered now by a solid coating of three-deckers. I can remember, when Dorchester was annexed to Boston, sitting on a big stone which used to adorn the corner of our street, and meditating on the duties of a metropolitan; but never did I foresee that *rus* could be so completely, so calamitously digested in *urbe*. A like assimilation is in process for Brighton and Hyde Park — yea, for Brookline, too, sturdily though she maintain her independence in the coils of the enveloping monster.

Most of all do I regret the downfall of suburban Roxbury, including Jamaica Plain, once the sylvan abode of fairies and fauns — disturbed, to be sure, but not dismayed by an omnipresent odor of breweries. Now Pan and his train have retreated in ever-widening circles; to catch a glimpse — merely a fleeting glimpse — of the wood-gods, one must push on to Dedham, to Needham, to Wellesley, to Weston, to Concord, to Bedford, to Woburn, to Stoneham.

Roxbury was my home for five years of the most romantic period, from eleven to sixteen. I knew all the poetry of its groves, its absurd rocks, its incredible cliffs. On Parker Hill, before the digging of the old reservoir that has recently been filled up, I hunted Indians. I discovered and explored the land of enchantment that is now Franklin Park. I shuddered at Bussey's Woods, scene of a horrid murder which I always identified with the story of the Babes in the Wood. At present that ill-famed grove is the darkly beautiful Hemlock Hill of the Arnold Arboretum; but it still looks like a peculiarly favorable spot for a crime, and I advise anyone contemplating murder to consider its advantages before choosing any other site. Then, too, I invented history for the unexplained Echo Chimney, majestic, mysterious on its lonely ledge. And I viewed the world from Fort Hill, beside the Standpipe, the rallying-place of our gang.

Down Fort Hill, with its long, steep, dangerously right-angled incline, I used to coast in winter, in preference to the more frequented Honeysuckle Hill. There it was that Jimmy Burns involuntarily saved my life; for at the perilous corner of the coast, my sled, which had skidded on the ice, ran into his, and was thereby prevented from plunging over a precipice fifty feet high. To me it was evident that Jimmy had been foreordained to perform this service, that such was the real purpose of his seemingly meaningless existence; but I never could bring him to look upon the incident in that light. Indeed, to him a trifling bruise on his thigh, where my runner struck him, looked more important than my salvation. The stone tablet subsequently erected on the summit of the hill, however, commemorated not this momentous episode, but something or other connected with the siege of Boston; and a whole line of its inscription had to be cut out and done over, because "siege" was misspelled.

Peculiarly sacred in my eyes was Day's Woods, out on Heath Street, toward Brookline Village. It was a soul-satisfying combination of verdure and sightly rock; and at its highest point, far in the interior, where we seldom penetrated, was perched a strange, silent, shuttered house, said to be haunted. To this grove, every spring, I betook myself, not, indeed, to hang wreaths upon its oaks, but to pluck violets. Some of the plants I transported to my own garden, where, under the influence of unaccustomed luxury, they developed into peculiar vegetables, all leaves and no flowers. So it often fares with adopted children. Today, on the site of Day's Woods, there is nothing but a vast, hideous hole in the ground. The place has long been used as a quarry, and is still thus exploited. A big schoolhouse has been constructed on one side, and the rest is gaping emptiness. For years, the haunted manor was left intact, solitary on a bare pinnacle, with everything around it excavated. A few bricks now are all that tell the tale.

Let us return to Chester Square; it is less depressing. I once lived close by, in a boarding-house on the Park, at the corner of Shawmut Avenue. There are few parts of Boston where I have not dwelt at one time or another. Twice has Dorchester claimed me, twice Roxbury, twice Brookline Street, once Washington Street, once Chester Park, once each, Chauncy and Mt. Vernon Streets. It was from Chauncy, then a road of residences with tiny areas in front, that I saw the great Boston fire; in fact, we were in the thick of it — bells, panic, smoke, heat, blazing embers pelting down on our woodshed, and no means of escape, because all the horses in the city were sick. We were saved only by a turn of the wind.

The Chester Park establishment was very select; there

cannot have been more than eight or nine boarders, although the house was large. Among them, I remember, were two vivacious young gentlemen, agents for two rival sewing-machine companies, who could be trusted, with their merry gibes at each other's expense, always to sustain conversation. Indeed, there was no lack of topics. I do not know whether it was really an *annus mirabilis* or whether it was only my first experience of daily contact with current news. There was the Chicago fire, the murder of Jim Fisk, and the Beecher scandal. The newspaper reports of this great trial furnished our table-talk not only with endless savory tidbits of gossip, but also with a stock of set phrases, which became the slang of the day. For instance, to the question, "How do you do?" the prescribed answer was, "Dear father, I feel so-so," this, according to a watchful housemaid's testimony, having been Mrs. Tilton's reply to her pastor's parochial inquiry. I matured fast during that year.

Our household differed from the boarding-house of facetious tradition in that, instead of a landlady, we had a landlord. Yes, the proprietor himself presided, suave and dignified. I cannot recall whether there was a Mrs., but I do remember that Mr. Atkinson was the Arthur of our Round Table. He was a distinguished-looking gentleman, with his black velvet jacket and his elegant black side-whiskers. His place of business (he was a grocer) was not far off, in a marble-faced building around the corner, on Washington Street; hence the possibility of his presence with us. Perhaps I do not interpret aright the feelings of my commensals; but it seems to me we regarded him as I suppose tenants, in the good old worshipful days, regarded their Squire. Whatever matters, profane or sacred, might form the theme of our unending pleasantries, the food set before us was never one of them. I cannot recollect much about the fare, for in those days I took little interest in the fleshpots; but I dare say it did not lend itself to trifling.

One of the supremely joyful moments of my childhood — one of my high lights of happiness — is connected with Chester Park. It is to be rated perhaps next to that witching and witchful evening on Sharon Street. A boy whom I knew went away for the afternoon and lent me his tricycle. O! the sense of speed, of ease, of mastery, as I propelled myself over the sidewalk, round and round the block, past Mr. Atkinson's grocery and back to his house! If the aviator knows the rapture of rapidity, I envy him not; for I know it, too. That little red tricycle was never at my disposal again, but the memory of it will abide forever.

Another pleasure of that season was the perusal of *Pickwick Papers*. I always remember my various habitations by the books I read in them. Then it was, too, that I wrote my first and only play, a comedy never contaminated by the effluvium of the footlights. Geography also revealed its charms, especially map-making, at which I became fairly proficient. Once, however, my pride had a bad tumble. I had finished a chart of our eastern states and the neighboring waters, and was just putting in the final lettering, which was my particular delight. Last of all, in full capitals, curving around the coast, was ATLANTIC OCEAN, executed in my best style. Not until I had completed the inscription, and was gazing at it, no doubt, with sinful satisfaction, did I see what had happened. Instead of ATLANTIC OCEAN — such was the all-pervasive, all-subduing influence of the black-whiskered master of the house — I had printed ATKINSON OCEAN.

These things savor of school; and, indeed, I did attend classes in the intervals between maladies. This time it was the Dwight School, where I suffered less than I did in most of my early scholastic retreats; for I cordially liked my teacher, I shared with the other boys an almost uncomfortable respect for our wise and stately principal, Mr. Page, and I made the acquaintance of some congenial spirits. Somehow I just failed to meet the most famous alumnus of the school, John L. Sullivan, who, I think, was my contemporary there, but never in my class. He could not stand it very long. There was indeed small chance for sport. The crowded little sunken yard was paved with brick, a fall meant sore knees for a fortnight, and one could hardly move without knocking somebody over. Mr. Page, to be sure, in his kindness tried to make play by tossing a ball for the boys to catch and return to him; but any competition was fraught with peril, and I was not to be lured from the corner of a doorway where I stood safely snuggled, counting the minutes until recess should be done.

Anyhow, the City Hospital was not far off. If you followed Chester Park to the eastward, you came pretty close to it, although the next street takes you nearer. The cross streets in that quarter — Chester, Worcester, Springfield, Dedham, Newton, Brookline, Canton, Dover, Gardner, and so on — are named after towns, as I one day, to my amazement, discovered. An alphabetical sequence is discernible in Brookline, Canton, Dedham, but no further. Strange phenomena abound in the South End. There I saw a great stone church sawed in two, and one half of it taken away. There was the City Hospital: why did it look so much like the State House, and how could one tell which was which? Then there was my

Uncle B.'s apartment house — the eighth wonder of the universe.

My uncle had dwelt for unknown eons in an ordinary dwelling at the corner of Tremont and Worcester Streets. There, year by year, he had entertained us at Thanksgiving. I did not enjoy these occasions, partly because of the tardy hour of the meal, partly because the house had a dark basement dining-room and depressingly dark red napkins, but mainly because my Uncle B. always kissed me. I liked my Uncle B., but I did not like to be kissed, especially by the stubby-faced sex. Sometimes I hoped he would forget; but no! he might forget other things, not that. Well, after this life had gone on for ages and ages and ages, my uncle did a wonderful thing. He bought Dr. Ivy's house, next door, and made over those two dwellings into an apartment house. It was asserted and firmly believed in the family that the resulting structure, The Worcester, was the first apartment house in Boston. I now have learned better; but, anyhow, it was one of the first, and it was the very first to impress itself on my consciousness. There were of course vast difficulties in the way. Dr. Ivy's home, which he had long wanted to sell, suddenly became very dear to him. I remember the Doctor as an elderly gentleman with a big top hat, a wig, a cane, a smooth face, and a benevolent expression; he was said to be a Perfectionist. At last, however, the house was acquired, and the stately pile erected. Six apartments! and two shops underneath! The Worcester may still be seen at the old stand, opposite the church; but one has to look sharp to pick it out. I am not calling attention to it for business reasons. Many years ago it passed out of the clan.

Other wonders are continually cropping up. Of late

years, now and then, I have come upon a curious building. The encounter is always accidental and unexpected — at least, as far as I am concerned; but it has been frequent enough to leave a distinct impress on my mind. I am disposed to think that the phenomenon is an objective reality, and that the house in question is there all the time, instead of popping into mundane existence, like Germelshausen, at stated intervals. I have even assured myself approximately of its habitat, narrowing the circle year by year, like a sheriff's posse around an entrapped but dangerous criminal. Its abode is a short cross-street not far below Dover. The house is either an antique structure remodeled or an imitation thereof — a small, low, brick building of Colonial type, plain but well proportioned, charming amidst its vulgar companions. The roof has surely been renewed; and above the entrance is a diminutive bay window, just big enough to hold a couple of flower-pots. On the door a brass plate bears the title, "Hawthorne Club." The brilliancy of the brass, the freshness of the flowers in the two pots, the general tidiness of the place betoken constant care, doubtless by spirit hands, for naught human have I ever beheld therein. Often have I questioned my acquaintances about the Club — cautiously, of course, always mindful of its possible unreality; but never have I got a satisfactory answer. Nearly all have disclaimed any knowledge whatever. A few antiquarians have hesitatingly and evasively admitted that they had heard of such a thing: some of these had an air of knowing considerably more than they cared to tell; others, on the contrary, seemed to me to be telling more than they knew. At any rate, the business is still shrouded in mystery; and, on the whole, I am glad to leave it thus enveloped.

Not less perplexing than a sudden emergence into the field of consciousness is total and unaccountable disappearance. There used to be a street, off Washington, in the lower South End, called Indiana Place. It was a narrow, murky street, as I remember it, with a quirk at the end. In the quirk was a kirk, and thither, of a Sunday, my mother used to take me to hear James Freeman Clarke, before the original Church of the Disciples was built on Brookline Street. Now, the strange thing is that no Indiana Place exists. Of this I am sure. I have tried it again and again, walking both ways along Washington Street — not simultaneously, of course, but alternately. I have even started from our old home on Brookline and tried to retrace our route, with my eyes half shut; and although I have run into a good many things and people, I have never run into Indiana Place. Every time, I find nothing but railway tracks in the spot where it ought to be. Curious happenings I have seen in my day: I have seen Shawmut Avenue break through into Tremont Street, I have seen Harrison Avenue reach out into an Extension, I have seen Fort Hill (the down-town one) dug away, I have seen Boston made bigger, better, and busier by the construction of a thoroughfare called Columbus Avenue, which for decades ended in a board fence; but nothing has happened so extraordinary as the evaporation of Indiana Place.

All that precedes has been leading up, stealthily but inevitably, to the feature which gives its title to this discourse. The Hawthorne Club has intermittently disclosed itself; Indiana Place, once familiar, has vanished forever; but there is in the South End a street which I saw but once, two years ago come Michaelmas. Really, I have no idea when Michaelmas is, but the expression lends an impressive preciseness to an otherwise unimpressive statement. Now, the extraordinary thing about this street is not that I should have seen it only once; for, to tell the truth, I have never looked for it again. No, its distinction lies in no quality of elusiveness or of obtrusiveness, but simply in its name. It is called Ivanhoe Street. There is no mistaking it; a large, clearly lettered sign, appropriately affixed at the corner, proclaims its identity. This fact in itself, in a city so secretive concerning the names of its thoroughfares, awakens attention.

But when your attention is awakened, it may only yawn and remark: "Why not? A good many other streets have self-expressive labels, immodest though such exposure may seem to good Bostonians. Why should not this one reveal itself? And if, as is probable, it was planned in the romantic sixties, what is more natural than that it should be christened after a favorite romantic hero?" Ah! that is the point. The street under discussion is not romantic, it is not genteel, it is not even presentable, and never was, although its respectability need not be called into question. To speak plainly, it is a back alley.

Now, some back alleys are the result of tragic downfall or of gradually erosive degeneration. They were once rustic roads, proud with pastures, decked with dwellings; or haply they were ancient urban streets, now too narrow for urban traffic, crushed between insurgent mountains of masonry. Not so the alley of the name of Ivanhoe. This one was conceived and born an alley, and never by any chance could have been aught else. In the swell-fronted South End, the blocks are laid out according to a foreordained pattern. Back to back, but a long distance apart, are two rows of deep houses. Behind the houses are back yards, of a length proportionate to the depth of the houses. And behind the back fences of the back yards runs an alley of sufficient width to admit a tipcart, these hidden routes being intestines for the discharge of refuse. Ash-barrels and garbage-pails border their sides, and the scattered contents of these receptacles all too frequently bestrew the roadway. Such an alley is Ivanhoe Street; one of the widest and one of the cleanest, but an alley, a predestined alley.

To be sure, modern congestion has introduced into the picture a row or two of little houses encroaching on the back yards and facing the alleyway. Can they have brought with them the romantic appellation? Did they, when they invaded the intestinal tract, attempt to veil their posteriority under the proud name of Ivanhoe? Or were they attracted by the name, bestowed on the alley at its birth by some absent-minded fairy godmother? Who can tell? Perhaps somebody can; but I hope he will not, for there is more profit in speculation than in knowledge.

I am aware that Max Beerbohm, in his treatise on "The Naming of Streets," professes skepticism regarding the profound significance of their titles. Can such disbelief be genuine? Can such a philosopher as Beerbohm must be (else he were not what he is, the cleverest of essayists) — can a modern philosopher, I say, habitually and constantly doubt that which a medieval philosopher never doubted for a moment, that *nomina sunt consequentia rerum?* No: an inherent connection there must be, though possibly concealed from our ken. Let us proceed, then, in the good old medieval way, beginning, not with inquiry at City Hall, but with the most abstract proposition applicable to the case, and working down to the proximity of concreteness. This is still, I believe, the method of logic; and it is manifestly the right one, because it allows no possibility to escape.

The name Ivanhoe, then, must have been imposed by an agency either superhuman or human. If by the former, it is useless to seek the wherefore, because no created intelligence can fathom the decrees of Providence. Let us assume, therefore, that the human mind is responsible, since this alternative alone admits of continued development. Next, the question arises: was the act intentional or unintentional? Did some one (for the idea must have originated in an individual consciousness), being sober and of sound mind, bequeath the title; or did it grow up casually, unrecorded, until it had fastened itself by tradition, after the fashion of Perkins Pond, Hiram's Hill, or Betty's Bend? The more one examines the second supposition, the less acceptable it becomes; for, whereas Hiram's Hill was undoubtedly so designated in the first place because it was owned or inhabited by a person called Hiram, it is in the highest degree improbable that Ivanhoe Street was ever the property or the abode of Ivanhoe. Should anyone wish to contest this statement, I am prepared to argue it further. If not, I pass on.

You observed, no doubt, the qualification, "being sober and of sound mind," and you may be disposed to reject it, on the assumption that the nomenclature under discussion may easily enough have been the work of an inebriate or a madman. Your objection is overruled on two grounds: firstly, while admitting that such a name as Ivanhoe may have been flung at an unoffending alley by a drunken or crazy man, I deny *in toto* the contention that the epithet would have been retained, adopted, and consecrated in a tablet by a community for the most part sane and dry; secondly, an acceptance of the theory of such irresponsible christening would preclude further investigation, inasmuch as the motives of maniacs and in-

toxicated people, like those of the Deity, are unfathom-
able.

Being reduced by logical process to the conclusion that
the name Ivanhoe was wittingly bestowed by a sane and
sober human being, we have only to determine his reason
for so doing. Here again we have a choice between two
hypotheses: his purpose was either bad or good. I put
"bad" first, because evil predominates in mankind. Assuming that his intention was malicious, against whom
was his malice directed? Did he mean to make mock of
Sir Walter Scott's hero by attaching his title to an inconspicuous back lane? Evidently not; for Ivanhoe, being
dead, could not have been harmed thereby. Or was it his
idea to hold the alley up to ridicule by coupling with it an
appellation so grandiose as to accentuate its own poverty?
Let us consider this suggestion. Either the godfather
lived in the alley or he did not. If he did not, would the
denizens or owners thereof have allowed him to afflict
their residence or property with a derisive name? Surely
not. If, on the other hand, he was an inhabitant of the
alley, he must have seen that his destructive enterprise
would involve himself, like Samson, in the ruin of his
temple. Such desperation, though not unparalleled, is so
rare as to make the supposition excessively unlikely.

It must be conceded, however, that we have now come
to a pass where we must deal no longer with certainties,
but with probabilities. On the one hand, we must imagine
a cynic so embittered, so frenzied, so lost to shame, as
to be willing, nay, eager, to bring everlasting contumely
upon his own street and incidentally upon himself. On
the other, let us picture a simple-minded philanthropist,
perhaps a street-lover, who wishes to endow a poor
thoroughfare with the best that he can give. And what is

better than a good name? For my part, I do not hesitate.
Possibly I am inclined to think more kindly of my fellow-
creatures than they deserve; but my vote, such as it is,
goes to the philanthropist. Whatever the sneering caviler
may assert, such little deeds of love are by no means un-
common. Think of the oft-cited gentleman who gave to
mis'ry (all he had) a tear. Assuredly such a name as Ivanhoe is worth more than a tear; and if the donor of the latter acquired in exchange a friend, it is fair to hope that
our generous patron gained, not one friend, but many,
presumably all the abutters on the alley. Think of the
much-advertised widow's mite, and reflect how modest
is the renown which our sponsor — perhaps himself a
widower — has won by his really more valuable contribu-
tion. As far as I know, this is his very first appearance in
literature. To give the best that one has, freely, not car-
ing how poor the gift may be in the sight of others: such
was the offering made by the sympathetic Jongleur de
Notre Dame and (less successfully, to be sure) by the un-
sympathetic Cain.

On the broad Damariscotta River, from South Bristol
and East Boothbay to the headwater town of Damariscotta, and back, there used to run a small steamer called
the "Anodyne." A convenient little craft she was, cover-
ing a route that no railway paralleled, and affording a
soothing, somnolent sail to those who took the trip for the
mere pleasure of it. No speed-boat was she, to transform
the scenery into an indiscriminate, uninteresting blur; the
passenger on the Anodyne saw all that was to be seen, and
saw it in comfort, lazily camped in the sunshine. In my
first acquaintance with the Anodyne I assumed that she
was so called for her soporific medicinal effect on her cus-
tomers. Finally, however, I was prompted to question

her captain, who told me the true story. "No, I gave her that name because I was sort o' fond of it," he said. "I ain't always been a skipper. For years and years, when I was young, I was a peddler, and I used to go a-peddlin' up and down this river. What I peddled was an Anodyne Liniment, and I can tell you it was great stuff; it sold good, too. Well, after a while I saved up enough money to buy this boat, and I've been a-runnin' her ever since. When I come to give her a name, I thought that seein' it was the Anodyne's money that bought her, it was only fair to call her the Anodyne. So Anodyne she is, and Anodyne she will always be."

I wish I could give an equally satisfying elucidation of the name of another boat, which I saw lying at a wharf in East Boothbay. Really, she suggested, and more acutely, the same problem of motive that was imposed by Ivanhoe Street. A most disreputable old tub, a mudscow, and a dilapidated one at that, paintless, gaping, dirt-plastered. And her name, inscribed in big letters on the stern, was "Evelyn Nesbit Thaw." Of the sundry and divergent explanations that present themselves, the one I prefer is this. A simple boatman, hirsute and hispid, by laborious economy has saved a few dollars, but, instead of purchasing a craft, seeks his anodyne in a week's metropolitan dissipation. His inquiry, "What's the best show in town?" receives the prompt answer, "Florodora." There, on the stage, with five other nymphs, he beholds her whose image forever after shall haunt him. Her name, grown faint perhaps in his memory, is revived by his indignant perusal of the newspapers, what time they are full to overflowing with the malodorous testimony elicited by the trial of her husband for the murder of the great architect. A staunch defender, an unknown, humble admirer, hopelessly far away, "earthworm in love with a star," as Victor Hugo puts it, he pays her the tribute of naming after her his most precious possession — his mudscow.

One more example, which brings us back to the vicinity of Boston. For Boston is justly famous for her beaches; and it was on one of them, Revere Beach, that I saw the cottage. Revere Beach is not only a very beautiful crescent-shaped expanse of hard sand; it is also a compactly popular resort. All day long, in the hot season, the shore is completely covered by swarms of people baking themselves in the sunshine. At the close of summer, their negroid bodies must show, somewhere about the middle, a ring of white betraying the habitual whereabouts of their bathing-suits. Just behind the strand, across the street, is a string of booths and shows of the familiar sort, and, where they cease, a long row of cottages. Many of these æstival habitations look like the shanties I used to build, in my boyhood, out of old scraps of wood and tarred paper. But every one of them has a name — sometimes a woman's, sometimes a town's, oftenest a flight of fancy, such as Heart's Delight, Garden of the Gods, Earthly Paradise, Our Summer Home. As I walk along, sympathetically inspecting these evidences of sentiment, I suddenly come to a halt, opposite a hut that is perhaps the scrappiest and scrawniest of them all. For above its door I read: "Dolce Stil Nuovo." In the name of the divine poet, what have we here? Some lowly compatriot of Alighieri, who vaunts his allegiance by christening his cot, with more enthusiasm than congruence, after the first product of his nation's greatest genius? Or perhaps some pale student, some struggling would-be poet, who sighs into the inscription over his portal the aspiration of his stunted existence? Neither. As the dwellers emerge into view, ready for their daily sun-bath, I can see that they are neither pale students nor countrymen of Dante. They are well nourished, they are jolly, they are red-headed, they are numerous — so numerous, issuing from their little cabin, that they suggest the endless ribbon flowing from the conjurer's mouth. Their speech bewrayeth them as followers of St. Patrick. There is only one possible explanation, and that one I hate to set before you. These good people, having picked up somewhere the phrase "Dolce far niente," and marked it as an appropriate designation of their seashore residence, had unfortunately, before they could put their design into effect, heard another Italian expression with the same beginning and the same cadence, which had supplanted the first.

What a difference a word will make, even a very little word! Long, long ago, on this same Revere Beach, not yet a public reservation, I used to patronize a bath-house which prominently displayed the following notice: "Gents intending to bathe will please leave their valuables to the Office." Now, if you consider it carefully, you will see that the above rather chilling admonition is not a prayer for a legacy; nor is it a warning that for gents to bathe is a dangerous indulgence: it is simply an offer of security for personal property. One had, indeed, to repose in the Office and the presiding Official a confidence which their appearance scarcely justified; but, after all, it seemed a bit safer than concealing your watch in one shoe and your pocketbook in the other, these hiding-places being a too generally accepted convention of the swimming-hole. Most of us, therefore, left our valuables (if we had any) "to the Office."

Words, idle words! I know not what they mean. The

characteristic idle word of the Spaniard is said to be
mañana. In Italy, the favorite expression is *subito*. Now,
mañana and *subito* would seem to have nothing in common, etymologically, acoustically, or visually; but they
signify exactly the same thing. Both of them stand for
the Greek Kalends. Along the coast of Maine, I have observed that the phrase nearest in function to *mañana* and
subito is "the fust o' the week"— "I'll try to get round
to it the fust o' the week," for example. "The fust o' the
week," to be sure, has not the remoteness of *mañana* and
subito; for although to the uninitiated its message may
appear vague, one discovers by experience that it repre-
sents something fairly definite. In theory, "the fust o'
the week" means Tuesday; in practice, among punctilious
people, it means Wednesday. It may be called, then, a
mild euphemism, as compared with the infinite euphemism of *mañana* and *subito*.

From their outlook on futurity one may conjecture the
various peoples' estimate of time. Around the Mediterranean, time has no value whatever. It is the one thing
with which a man may be lavish, the one thing which
everybody may throw away, the one thing which rich and
poor share alike. Further north, in Germany and France
and England, time begins to have a price — not an exorbitant price, to be sure, but a respectable valuation.
To find the commodity at the top notch of inflation, one
must come to America. For us, time is immeasurably
more precious than any other possession. We care more
for it than for lands or gold or health or power; we think
of time so constantly that we never have a moment left
to think of eternity. Wasting a minute is like throwing
away an ounce of radium. Our whole lives are passed in
transition, in speeding from one station to another, with

minds intent, not on the station of our present endeavor, but on our chances of making the next one; our nervous energy is all spent in worrying lest we miss a connection. It is only in idyllic regions still uninfected by the national mania that one encounters the innocent duplicity of such a phrase as "the fust o' the week."

Still, as long as anywhere among us there shall linger a lotus-land whose future lies in the hazy first of the week and whose enchanted boat of life bears the name of Anodyne; as long as the dwellers on our temporary Typees shall cherish even a clouded concept of *dolce far niente;* as long as our mudscowmen shall be led through life by the ideal of a Princesse Lointaine; as long as our street-sponsors shall wed past to present, romance to reality — so long may we poor city rats, hurried and harried though we be, find an hour to waste in idle speculation about Ivanhoe and his street.